# THE CITY OF YORK

## A Masonic Guide

# Dedication

*In loving memory of O'*

# THE CITY OF YORK

# YORK

## A Masonic Guide

## David Harrison

Lewis Masonic

First published 2016

ISBN 978 0 85318 520 8

Published by Lewis Masonic

an imprint of Ian Allan Publishing Ltd, Addlestone, Surrey KT15 2SF.
Printed in Wales.

Visit the Lewis Masonic website at www.lewismasonic.co.uk

# CONTENTS

# Abbreviations

AQC    Transactions of the Ars Quatuor
       Coronatorum
DCRO   Durham County Record Office
JCRFF  The Journal for the Centre of
       Research into Freemasonry and
       Fraternalism
JIVR   The Journal of the Institute of
       Volunteering Research
LCHS   The Transactions of the Lancashire
       and Cheshire Historical Society
THSLC  Transactions of the Historic Society
       of Lancashire and Cheshire
UGLE   The United Grand Lodge of England

# Acknowledgements

I would like to thank a number of people for their help during my research for this book; first and foremost Dave Taylor and David Hughes for their assistance in giving me access to the York Grand Lodge documents, rolls and minute books, along with the artefacts of the York Grand Lodge. Thanks are also given to Martin Cherry from the Library and Archives of the UGLE, Keith Hatton from Jerusalem Preceptory No. 5 for giving access to their early records and Martin Faulks at Lewis Masonic. I would also like to mention York Masonic historian Neville Barker Cryer whose valuable research continues to inspire. All photographs were taken by the author unless otherwise stated.

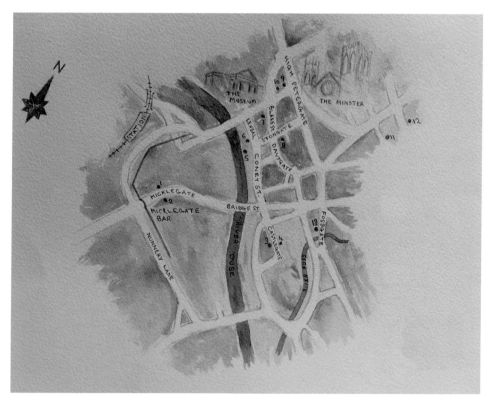

# INTRODUCTION

York in the eighteenth century was seen as the ancient centre of England, and in Masonic terms, this ancient northern city had its own independent Grand Lodge that rivalled the Grand Lodge in London. Indeed, York is now celebrated around the Masonic world, especially with the York Rite in the US, and there are a number of lodges in the US that celebrate York Masonry, such as the Ancient York Lodge which meets in Massachusetts[1] and another Ancient York Lodge which meets in New Hampshire.[2] York Masonry is also held in high regard in some Latin American countries such as Mexico, which has the York Grand Lodge of Mexico[3] and also in Bolivia.[4] There are records that refer to speculative Freemasonry in York and in Yorkshire dating to the 1600s, and this book aims to give a street-by-street guide to all things Masonic within the ancient Roman city, while also referring to the larger county as a whole.

**Key to map opposite**

1 No 85 Micklegate, town house of Charles Bathurst
2 Holy Trinity
3 Castlegate House
4 Fairfax House
5 Guildhall
6 Mansion House
7 Assembly Rooms
8 Punch Bowl
9 Duncombe Place Masonic Hall
10 Theatre Royal
11 Bedern Hall
12 Merchant Taylors
13 Merchant Adventurers' Hall

For example, there are a number of different and fascinating ritual variations, the York Working nd the Humber Use; both have noted elements that date to the eighteenth century.

There are literally thousands of Masonic references to be found in the ancient city of York; from the mysterious medieval Masons loft in the Minster (which incidentally has hundreds of masons marks, Masonic stain glass windows and Masonic symbols on display) to the beautiful Masonic Hall at Duncombe Place. York has traces of Freemasonry in abundance; Duncombe Place is also the location of all the rare manuscripts for the Grand Lodge of All England held at York, and this new Masonic guide book of York will include never-before-seen photos of the rolls, manuscripts and artefacts of this early independent Grand Lodge.

The book will look at old pubs and places where the ancient St. John's Lodges met, such as the Merchant Adventurers' Hall and the Punch Bowl Tavern, and the early Masonic symbolism that decorates some of the beautiful Georgian town houses of York, many of which had links to famous Freemasons of the day such as Sir Robert Fairfax and Charles Bathurst. The work will act as a companion piece to *The City of London: A Masonic Guide*\*, and is both educational and entertaining; filled with new photos and easy-to-understand references and map, all aimed at assisting the reader in discovering the Masonic mysteries of York and the county of Yorkshire, both from the past and the present.

\*Published by Lewis Masonic, 2006

# YORK AS THE ANCIENT CENTRE OF NORTHERN ENGLAND

York, known as *Eboracum* in Roman times, was the capital of the province of Britannia Inferior, the northern part of Roman Britain, and the city played a vital role in the history of the Roman Empire when Constantine the Great was proclaimed Emperor by the troops based in the fort in AD 306. After the decline of Roman Britain, the old Roman fort became the centre for King Edwin of Northumbria in the early seventh century. By the ninth century, the city was the centre of the Vikings, and their name for the city – Jórvik - later became reduced to York following the Norman Conquest. So York, in effect, had been the capital of northern England from the Roman era, through the Anglo-Saxon and Viking periods.

The York Grand Lodge rivalled itself with the London Modern or Premier Grand Lodge, and based its ancient foundation on the tradition that the Anglo-Saxon Prince Edwin held the first Assembly of Masons in York in AD 926. There is no existing evidence for Prince Edwin's York Masonic Assembly, and many Masonic writers and historians, such as Arthur Edward Waite, dismissed the event as pure legend. Waite did acknowledge that a Prince Edwin existed in relation to King Athelstan, dating to around the time of the early tenth century, as there was an Edwin who appeared as a witness to Athelstan's signature on an extant charter at Winchester. The Anglo-Saxon scribe Bede does write of King Edwin of Northumbria being baptised at York Cathedral in 627 and mentions the rebuilding which took place at this time. Indeed, this reference may have influenced Dr Francis Drake when he presented a date 'about the Six Hundredth Year after Christ' for Edwin as 'Grand Master' in York, when he gave his famous speech at the Merchant Adventurers' Hall in 1726. Drake was presenting King Edwin as the great Anglo-Saxon ruler of All England, harking back to a time when Northumbria was a powerful Anglo-Saxon kingdom, a kingdom that spawned other mighty leaders during the seventh century such as King Oswald.[5] This is the vision that Drake held when he put forward the title of the *Grand Lodge of all England*; a title that reflected powerful ancient roots, not just in Freemasonry but also in the history of York itself.[6]

The stance of the York Grand Lodge was clear; York was the ancient northern capital, and they had an ancient right as a Grand Lodge. Francis Drake reiterated this stance when he wrote *Eboracum* in 1736, a somewhat hefty book of around 800 pages with the rather long subtitle of *The History and Antiquities of the City of York, from its Original to the Present Time; together with the History of the Cathedral Church and the Lives of the Archbishops of that See*, was finally published in 1736. There were 540 subscribers – a number of whom were members of the York Grand Lodge; good old Masonic networking providing some fine support. Elements of the work reflected the themes found in his speech to the Merchants Adventurers' Hall ten years earlier, with the importance of the history of York – architecturally and culturally – being

*Dr Francis Drake, Grand Master of the York Grand Lodge in 1761. The print is taken from* **Eboracum.** (Courtesy of the York Lodge library, Duncombe Place)

strongly put forward throughout. York was a cultural rival to London, and for Drake, there was no doubting that.

Indeed, Drake confidently guaranteed his readers that 'There is no place out of London, so polite and elegant to live in as the City of York.'[7] The work also criticised how London came into prominence under William the Conqueror. Drake writing how York was ravaged under the 'Tyrant' who subjected his own people to 'the greatest slavery'; the once superior Roman city becoming the second city of the kingdom – a theme that was certainly reflected in the treatment of the York Grand Lodge by its London rival.[8] York was indeed a thriving cultural centre of the north; during the eighteenth century, York becoming renowned for its Georgian architecture and its cultured social scene became attractive to the visiting Scottish nobility. The York races became an important attraction, the ancient city having many fine Inns to accommodate visitors, and it cultivated an intellectual scene, with scientists such as John Goodricke, artists such as Thomas Beckwith, actors such as Tate Wilkinson and Bridge Frodsham and writers such as Dr Francis Drake and Dr John Burton.[9]

The York Grand Lodge attracted many writers after its demise at the close of the eighteenth century in an effort to investigate its origins and mysteries, these writers doing much to inspire later Masonic researchers. One such writer was Godfrey Higgins; a Freemason, social reformer and radical writer of religious works, the most renowned of these works being *Anacalypsis*, which was published posthumously in 1836. Higgins was a member of the prestigious London based Prince of Wales Lodge, which boasted such members as Prime Minister George Canning and of course the Prince of Wales. He had visited the last Grand Secretary of the York Grand Lodge – William Blanchard, owner of the *York Chronicle* – and mentions in *Anacalypsis* that he had seen certain documents, particularly describing the 'Old Charges' that would later become known as the York MS No. 1. He discusses how it was written on the back of the parchment roll, that Francis

Drake had presented it to the York Grand Lodge, and that it had been found in Pontefract Castle, Higgins also putting forward that there was a tradition that the lodge records were sent to the castle during the Civil Wars.

Higgins also stated that he had passed the documents on to the Duke of Sussex, who was the Grand Master of the United Grand Lodge at the time of his writing, though it appears that it was only a copy that was presented to the Duke, as the original manuscript is still kept in York. According to Hughan in his *Old Charges,* a copy of the York MS No. 1 was made around 1830 by order of Bro. William Henry White, (The Grand Secretary of the time) but not being a perfect copy, another was copied by Bro. Robert Lemon, (Deputy Keeper of State Papers) and was presented to the Duke of Sussex. Both transcripts are still preserved; likewise a letter from the latter gentleman to the Duke, dated 9 September 1830, states that 'it might be interesting to collate the transcript, said by [William] Preston to be in the possession of the Lodge of Antiquity, with that from which the above is made.'[10]

Putting forward that the York Grand Lodge had older and more mystical origins, Higgins enigmatically stated that 'the presumption was pretty strong'; that the Druidical Lodge – a lodge that came under the sway of the York Grand Lodge that had been based in Rotherham – was the same as the Culdees of Monastica. He goes further to link the Masons of York to India;[11] his comments on the York Grand Lodge and his visit to Blanchard, were later discussed by the esoteric Masonic writer Arthur Edward Waite.[12] More recently, historian Andrew Prescott remarked that Higgins may have been an influence on Richard Carlile's version of the Masonic ritual which was published in his early nineteenth century exposé *Manual of Freemasonry*.[13] Other writers that visited William Blanchard, who became the last surviving member of the York Grand Lodge, included William Hargrove, who in 1819, claimed to have been shown documents that had once belonged to the York Grand Lodge by Blanchard, including the now lost final minute book of 1780-1792. Hargrove wrote the renowned *History and Description of the Ancient City of York* which was published in 1818,[14] and his visit to Blanchard, and the documents he witnessed, was referred to by later prominent Masonic writers such as Robert Freke Gould in his widely read *History of Freemasonry*,[15] and by the aforementioned Arthur Edward Waite, who both continued to research the importance of the York Grand Lodge.

*The Merchants Adventurers' Hall, scene of the famous speech by Dr Francis Drake on the 27th of December, 1726, and, for the first time, the use of the term Grand Lodge was used in relation to York.* Photo (https://commons.wikimedia.org/wiki/File:Merchant_Adventurers_Hall_1989.jpg) by Rodhullandemu/CC BY (https:creativecommons.org/licenses/by-sa/3.0/deed.en)

# AN INTRODUCTION TO THE GRAND LODGE OF ALL ENGLAND HELD AT YORK[16]

One of the first leading localities that declared itself independent from the 'Premier' Grand Lodge of England was York, and on the 27 December, 1726, during Drake's speech in the Merchants Adventurers' Hall, the new title of *Grand Lodge of all England held at York* was declared. York, like its other northern Roman City Chester, has a strong tradition of medieval Mystery Plays associated with the ancient city's trade guilds, and has possible early references to 'speculative' Freemasonry dating to the 1600s. Chester also has a number of early references to Freemasonry going back to the late seventeenth and early eighteenth centuries, and like York, all featuring prominent local families, merchants and tradesmen.[17]

The York Grand Lodge kept this traditional link to the Freemen merchants and tradesmen, for example a grocer named Seth Agar was made a Freeman in 1748, became Sheriff in 1760 and Grand Master of the York Grand Lodge in 1767. In 1693, a version of the 'Old Charges' mentions six people who were members of a Lodge in Yorkshire, and a mahogany flat rule, now held at the York Masonic Hall, displays Masonic symbols. Dating to 1663, it names three prominent York figures, including a certain John Drake, who seems to have been collated to the Prebendal Stall of Donnington in the Cathedral Church of York in October 1663. He was probably a relation of the aforementioned Francis Drake who was to be a prominent figure behind the later revival of the York Grand Lodge.

Though records reveal the York Grand Lodge was only officially named as such in 1726, perhaps as a reaction to the London based Premier/Modern Grand Lodge, Gould, in his *History of Freemasonry*, suggested that it had its foundations much earlier giving 1705 as a date in which the York Grand Lodge began, despite only meagre evidence. In 1725, however, it seems the York brethren began to use the term 'Grand Master' instead of 'President', and a year later, they claimed superiority over the Premier/Modern Grand Lodge of 1717, thus adding legitimacy to its status and producing the absolute title of the Grand Lodge of *all* England held at York.[18]

The power struggle that lay behind the formation of independent 'Grand Lodges' in the eighteenth century seems to reflect a strong reaction from a localised elite against the audacity of the London based Premier/Modern Grand Lodge. The York Grand Lodge was controlled by leading local gentlemen, such as Sir George Tempest Baronet, who is listed as being 'President' in 1705. Other examples of this powerful elite include the Right Honourable Robert Benson, Lord Mayor of York (later Baron Bingley) who is also listed as being 'President' in 1707, and Admiral Robert Fairfax, MP in 1713 and Mayor in 1715, who became Deputy President in 1721. The majority of the gentlemen and tradesmen involved in the Grand Lodge served in local government as Alderman, Mayor, Sheriff and as Members of Parliament for York and the surrounding area. These included Sir William Robbinson who was 'President' in 1708 and became MP for York in 1713, William Milner, who also served as a Member for York, and Edward Thompson Esq., who actually served as MP during his time as 'Grand Master' in 1729.[19]

This strong and close 'clique' of powerful local gentlemen seemed to rule the York Grand

Lodge completely in the early decades of the eighteenth century. The Freemen tradesmen within the York Grand Lodge also had family connections within Freemasonry; such as Leonard Smith, who was also an operative mason. His son followed his example and became an operative mason and a lodge member. John Whitehead, a Freeman Haberdasher who became Chamberlain in 1700 and Sheriff in 1717, was the great-great-great uncle of York Grand Lodge historian T. B. Whytehead. Other members who had relatives within the Grand Lodge include Thomas and Josiah Beckwith, George and John Palmes, and the aforementioned Francis Drake FRS, to name but a few.[20]

Despite this seemingly harmonious image of close family ties within the 'Grand Lodge' structure, it is interesting that Charles Fairfax, who held Jacobite sympathies, was fined and subsequently imprisoned for recusancy in 1715. His house was searched and his gun confiscated, and he was eventually brought before Robert Fairfax (who was Mayor at the time), Sir Walter Hawksworth and Sir William Robinson, all members of the old York Lodge. Another local gentleman present at Charles Fairfax's hearing was Sir Henry Goodricke, who married the daughter of another old York Lodge member, Tobias Jenkyns, who happened to be Mayor twice in 1701 and 1720. Jenkyns also served as MP for York in 1715, beating fellow candidate and old York Lodge member Sir William Robinson.[21]

Francis Drake also had Jacobite sympathies, though, as far as can be ascertained he did not become actively involved in any agitation.[22] However, his friend and associate Dr John Burton did become involved in Jacobite intrigues, being imprisoned for a time. A later visitor to the York Grand Lodge who held Jacobite sympathies was local Catholic and Freemason William Arundell, famous for removing the skulls of executed Jacobites from the pinnacles of Micklegate Bar in York in 1754. In his all-important speech to the Merchant Adventurers Hall in 1726, Drake commented that 'the whole Brotherhood may be called good

Christians, Loyal Subjects, and True Britons',[23] perhaps asserting that the York Brethren were as loyal as the staunch Hanoverian London based 'Modern' brethren. Despite this assertion, it is suspicious that the York Grand Lodge became quiet during the 1740s and 1750s, the period of the Jacobite uprising.[24]

Of all the local gentlemen involved in the York Grand Lodge, Drake was perhaps one of the most important. Drake was the son of a Yorkshire clergyman who had been the Vicar of Pontefract, and became involved in Freemasonry at an early age, being a passionate champion of the ancient traditions of the York Grand Lodge. Drake zealously expressed the mythical links with King Edwin's first Masonic assembly at York Cathedral.[25] He was critical of Desaguliers' and Anderson's changes to the Craft, and like his southern counterpart, William Preston, Drake was a historian, writing a *History of York* which was published in 1736. Drake also presented to the York Grand Lodge the Parchment Roll of Constitutions, which had been supposedly found during the demolition of Pontefract Castle, and would have given Drake increased status within the close circle of York Masons. Indeed, even in a mid-nineteenth century edition of Paine's *Origins of Freemasonry*, this document is mentioned in the preface of the work when the editor comments on rebellions and rivalries within Freemasonry:

'These two lodges (London and Scotland) soon began to quarrel about precedency; each endeavouring to prove its priority by existing records of labouring masons…established many centuries before. The Yorkites, it is believed produced the oldest documents.'[26]

Drake played a major role during the revival of the York Grand Lodge in 1761, being Grand Master until 1762. He died in 1771.[27]

The lack of official York Masonic records during the 1740s and 1750s has led Masonic historians of the nineteenth century, such as Gould, to suggest that the York Grand Lodge quickly went into decline. It has therefore been accepted that the York Grand Lodge became dormant during this period, but was hastily revived in 1761, when it became apparent that the Modern Grand Lodge of London had spread its influence and invaded the territory of the old York Grand Lodge. The founding of a Modern lodge by a company of actors within the city walls at a tavern called the Punch Bowl, seemed to have triggered a reaction from a small group of original York Grand Lodge Masons, who quickly ejected the 'Modern' lodge, replacing it with their own.[28]

The revival of the York Grand Lodge was the result of the involvement of six local gentlemen, led by Drake, and it soon began to flourish again, with ten lodges founded under its jurisdiction. Though during the official 're-launching' of the York Grand Lodge, a number of brethren were present from the usurped Modern lodge, some of whom had actually joined the re-launched York Grand Lodge. The majority of the new lodges were located in Yorkshire, but one lodge was founded in Lancashire, and another, the 'Duke of Devonshire', as far away as Macclesfield in Cheshire.

The Lancashire Lodge, situated in Hollinwood, near the cotton producing town of Oldham, was called the Lodge of Fortitude, and was mentioned in the minutes of the Oldham based Modern Lodge of Friendship. The minutes refer to various visiting brethren from the 'York' lodge attending the Oldham based Lodge of Friendship up until 1795, and various members of the 'York' lodge who were also members of the Modern lodge were mentioned into the early nineteenth century as being active in the Lodge of Friendship.[29] These visits provide an insight to the relationship between localised Modern lodges and 'York' lodges, reminding us that despite the antagonism between Grand Lodges, Freemasons from all backgrounds could still relate to each other at local level. The York Grand Lodge continued to include prominent

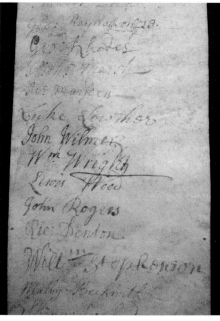

*A Roll listing the Master Masons of York, the name of Francis Drake can be seen in the bottom section of signatures.*

14

date, the surviving York Grand Lodge members, such as Blanchard, the Grand Chaplain Rev. John Parker, and the last Grand Master Edward Wolley, became increasingly involved with the 'Union' Lodge, finding sympathy in a lodge, which had been founded on the principles of union.

The York 'Union' Lodge was founded in York in 1777 by both Antient and Modern Freemasons and became a bastion to the memory of the York Grand Lodge.[31] The brethren were still using the York Working of the ritual in 1822, when the lodge finally agreed to adopt the new system, as taught by the Lodge of Reconciliation, which had been set up by the United Grand Lodge. Despite this, the 'Union' Lodge decided to continue the York Working as no member of the lodge had seen the new system demonstrated.[32] The York architectural historian John Browne, who joined the 'Union' Lodge in 1825, was heavily influenced by Antient York Masonry and studied the Antient ritual, ensuring that at least in part, it survived. The York Grand Lodge seemed unable to compete with the might of the Modern and Antient Grand Lodges, fading away in the opening years of the nineteenth century.[33] However, there are many places to see in York and the surrounding areas, that are associated with the York Grand Lodge, and each place has its own secret to reveal.

local gentlemen, such as William Siddall Esq., who served as Mayor the same year he served as Grand Master in 1783, Sir Thomas Gascoigne, Bart., and William Blanchard, who was Grand Secretary, and owned the York Chronicle.

Blanchard was also the custodian of the minutes and documents of the York Grand Lodge after its demise, and became the main source of information for Masonic historians in the early nineteenth century. Blanchard presented the Records of the York Grand Lodge to the York based 'Union' Lodge in 1837.[30] The York Grand Lodge continued officially until 1792, but as we shall see, it may have survived into the early years of the nineteenth century, though no documents are in existence to substantiate this, the last entry in the minute book being on the 23 August 1792. After this

# THE MYSTERIES OF MICKLEGATE

**Micklegate Bar**
The pinnacles of Micklegate Bar were where the heads of Jacobite traitors were displayed after the Jacobite rebellion of 1745. In 1754, a Freemason and a Catholic by the name of William Arundell removed the rotting skulls, and for his endeavours, he was tried at the Lent Assizes the following year, was convicted

and sentenced to two years imprisonment, fined £5.00, and required to obtain sureties for his future good behaviour for a further two years. In 1762, he was blackballed from joining the Punch Bowl Lodge – a lodge that came under the sway of the York Grand Lodge - though he visited the actual York Grand Lodge a number of times.[34]

Unlike the London and Scottish Grand Lodges, the York Grand Lodge went into hibernation during the 1740s and 1750s. York was however completely bypassed by the Jacobite forces, which passed through Carlisle in Cumberland, down through Preston and Manchester in Lancashire, and finally reached Derby before retreating back into Scotland using the same route.[35] The leaders of the community in York pledged allegiance to George II, but Dr Francis Drake was, at this time, undoubtedly the most influential of the York Grand Lodge members, and was an open Jacobite. His outspoken Tory associate Dr John Burton was also drawn into Jacobite intrigues, which, as we shall see, led to a set of events that was displayed in public. Perhaps with an overall downturn in Masonry and the overt Jacobite links that Drake displayed, it was enough for the staunchly independent York Grand Lodge to lay low for a while, re-emerging in 1761, with Drake at the helm.

## No. 86 Micklegate – the townhouse of the first York Grand Master, Charles Bathurst

Charles Bathurst Esq. was the first York Mason who held the title of Grand Master in 1725. He was baptised on the 1 October 1702, and on joining the York 'Grand Lodge' in July 1725, he replaced his father, who died in 1724 (Charles Bathurst who was listed as being a Grand President in 1724 was, according to York Masonic historian Whytehead, most

*The busy thoroughfare that is Micklegate Bar. Freemason and Catholic William Arundell removed the rotting skulls of Jacobites from here in 1754*

*The town house of Charles Bathurst in Micklegate. Bathurst was declared the first Grand Master in 1726*

probably his father). Bathurst Jnr became the first 'Grand Master' on the 27 December 1725. Bathurst resided in a Georgian Townhouse at No.86 Micklegate, and a clue to his father's probable membership is a symbol used within Freemasonry. Placed prominently on the downspout of the house; the Bathurst family crest included the image of a snake eating its own tail, otherwise known as the 'Ouroboros', representing eternity, a symbol which is still used in Freemasonry today, and is also featured as a prominent symbol in certain documents relating to the York 'Union' Lodge. His initials and those of his wife, Frances, are also on the downspouts. She was buried at St. Martin-cum-Gregory church across the road.

Micklegate was a prestigious location that attracted the affluent members of York society; it had been the Royal processional route into the city. In 1727, an image of Bathurst House was included on John Cossins' *New and Exact*

*Plan of the City of York* and, in 1736; Dr Francis Drake commented that 'very good new houses' occupied the route. Charles Bathurst Jnr died unmarried and the house became occupied by Abstrupus Danby, a local lawyer. The elegant townhouse of Charles Bathurst at Micklegate is worth seeing on your Masonic tour of York, especially as the Masonic symbol of the Ouroboros on display is arguably an excellent early example of prominent public Masonic symbolism.

Above: *The Ouroboros on the iron downspout of Charles Bathurst's town house in Micklegate.*

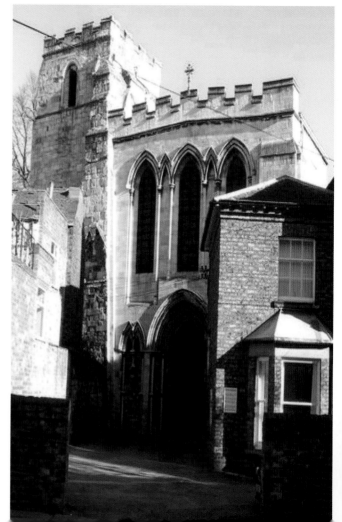

*Right: Holy Trinity Church, Micklegate, seen from Priory Street. The church itself is medieval and has a number of interesting stonemason's marks.*
Photo (https://commons. wikipedia.org/wiki/File:Holy_ Trinity_church_Micklegate_-_ geograph.org.uk_-_673484. jpg) by Gordon Hatton (http:// www.geograph.org.uk/ profile/4820) / CC BY (https:// creativecommons.org/licenses/ by-sa/2.0/deed/en)

### The monument to Dr John Burton, Holy Trinity Church at Micklegate

Dr John Burton was a very close friend and associate of Dr Francis Drake, and they both shared the same political ideology, both being Jacobites. Burton was born in Colchester on 9 June 1710, the son of a London merchant. After graduating from Cambridge in 1733, he continued his training in Leyden, Paris, and Rheims, where he obtained the degree of MD. He returned to England, settling in Wakefield after marrying Mary Henson in York Minster, and finally moved to York in 1738. The inventor of obstetric forceps, Burton was immortalised as Dr Slop in Laurence Sterne's *Tristram Shandy*, considered by many to be the first modern novel. Sterne, an Irish-born clergyman who settled in and around York, had active connections with the Minster throughout his life; his uncle the Rev. Jacques Sterne, the Precentor at the Minster, being Burton's most ardent opponent, and thus he would have obviously been aware of Burton's medical career and blatant Tory political leanings. Burton was an outspoken Tory; he was said to have actually met the Jacobite rebels near Settle during the 1745 rebellion and, on returning to York, he was imprisoned in the Castle gaol until March the following year, when he was sent to London to be placed under house arrest. It was here that he met Flora MacDonald, the young woman who aided Bonnie Prince Charlie to escape capture.[36]

It was his care for the poor and sick of York, which led to his scheme for the York County Hospital being founded in 1740, his friend Drake gaining his position there the following year. Despite being close to Drake and sharing the same Jacobite leanings, Burton was never a member of the York Grand Lodge, though his belief in the ethos of education and charity would have certainly been recognised there. Despite the damaging Jacobite ties, Burton, like Drake, went on to publish a well-respected medical work; *An Essay towards a complete new system of Midwifery* in 1751,[37] and like Drake, Burton had a passion for antiquarianism, publishing his *Monasticon Eboracense* in 1758. At least five of the 15 subscribers were York Grand Lodge Masons. Burton died in January 1771.

The church itself is medieval, and has a number of interesting stonemason's marks. It is mentioned in the Domesday Book of 1086, and having been destroyed when William the Conqueror 'wasted the North', it was given to the Abbot and Monks of St Martin's Abbey who rebuilt the church. In response to the dissolution of the monasteries by Henry VIII, the last prior, Robert Speight, took part in the Pilgrimage of Grace, though unlike the less fortunate abbots that took part, he survived and was buried in the choir in 1545. After the Reformation, the church was allowed to continue as a parish church, and after various alterations and the demolition of the old Priory gateway by the Goodricke family who owned a house on Micklegate, the church is still open for worship and is well worth a visit.

*The memorial for Dr John Burton, Holy Trinity, Micklegate.*

# TAVERNS, INNS, COFFEE HOUSES AND BOOKSELLERS ASSOCIATED WITH YORK FREEMASONRY

**The Punch Bowl Tavern, Stonegate** – location for the York Grand Lodge, the Punch Bowl Lodge and the French Prisoners of War Lodge, during the later eighteenth century

As we have seen, the York Grand Lodge was revived in 1761, and the founding of a lodge that met in the Punch Bowl Tavern under the 'Modern' Grand Lodge seemed to have been the catalyst, bringing six of the original York brethren back together to resurrect the Grand Lodge. Dr Francis Drake led these six brethren, and the revived Grand Lodge quickly expelled the 'Modern' lodge, replacing it with a lodge under the York Grand Lodge, which continued to meet in the Punch Bowl.[38]

During the 're-launching' of this newly revived Grand Lodge of All England held at York, a number of brethren were present from the usurped 'Modern' Punch Bowl lodge; the brethren having joined the York Grand Lodge. This new lodge under York did not last long however, and by January 1763, the lodge had closed. This revival and the events behind the 'hijacking' of the 'Modern' Punch Bowl lodge can best be seen in the official response to the Modern Grand Lodge which was proposed at a meeting in December 1767, after a number of letters had been received from London, addressed to the Punch Bowl lodge:

'That the Grand Secretary do inform the Grand Lodge in London that the Lodge heretofore held under their Constitution No.259... has been for some years discontinued and that the most antient Grand Lodge of All England held for time immemorial in this City is now the only Lodge held therein.'[39]

Another lodge under 'York', referred to as the French Prisoners of War lodge, was also held at the Punch Bowl, and was constituted on the 10 June 1762, for French brethren only. York was the residence of French prisoners during the Seven Years' war; some were granted parole and allowed the liberty of walking a mile around the city. However, the lodge was soon to end, as by April the following year the war was over, the prisoners left, and the lodge closed. The Punch Bowl however, is still going strong, and is well worth a visit to soak up the historical atmosphere and get a feeling of where these eighteenth century York Freemasons once met, drank and dined.

**The 'Printers Devil', No. 33 Stonegate: Bookshops, Printing Presses and Freemasons**
York certainly has some of the most eccentric and quirky architectural features in England and amongst the many shops and pubs of the Shambles and Stonegate, there are many hidden carved, decorative characters looking down on the unsuspecting visitor. Stonegate in York was once home to the book shops and printers of the city and here, perched cunningly above No.33 Stonegate is the famous 'Printers Devil' (named as the culprit for many a misspelling or error in a printed book). The Printers Devil along with the figure of Minerva, which is located above a shop on the corner of Petergate and Minster Gates, are a reminder that this area was indeed an intellectual centre, with leading Freemasons being involved as writers and printers. Indeed, many members of the York Grand Lodge and their circle published works; Dr Francis Drake, Dr John Burton, actor and theatre manager Tate Wilkinson[40] and William Blanchard all

*The Punch Bowl. The punch bowl itself was actually a symbol and beverage that was associated with the Whigs, the Tories being associated with claret*

published various works locally, revealing that York was a thriving cultural scene which attracted writers, artists and intellectuals. This tradition continued into the early nineteenth century, with local Masons such as John Browne and Godfrey Higgins writing renowned works.

*The York Courant* – an early York newspaper – started out in Stonegate in 1725, before moving to Coney Street, where in 1738, Caesar Ward took over the paper. Ward, a Tory, was a close friend and associate of York

*The Printers Devil, Stonegate.*

Grand Lodge stalwart Francis Drake; Drake along with others, helping Ward to re-establish running the paper after bankruptcy forced him to sell the printing house in 1745.[41] Between 1751 and 1760, with the assistance of Caesar Ward, Drake published the thirty volumes of *The Parliamentary or Constitutional History of England from the Earliest Times to the Restoration of King Charles II*, with a second edition, in twenty-four volumes, appearing in 1763.

William Blanchard - the last Secretary of the York Grand Lodge – was the proprietor of the *York Chronicle* for many years and printed many pamphlets, some for the Grand Lodge itself,[42] while other pamphlets were quite outspoken and verging on the radical, such as *The Defence of Prisoners in York Castle for not paying Tithes against the Charges of George Markham, Vicar of Carlton, in Yorkshire, contained in his Book, entitled "Truth for the Seekers"* in 1797, and *The Prisoners' Defence supported, by the Authors of the Defence*, which was printed the following year.[43] Blanchard however, was not the first to publish the paper; in 1772 the *York Chronicle* was established as a rival to the York Courant, the only newspaper then published in the city. Christopher Etherington, bookseller and publisher, at his press in Coppergate, published this new paper weekly and the first number appeared on the 18 December 1772, under the title of the *York Chronicle and Weekly Advertiser*. It was at first 'a quarto, containing four leaves' and had a somewhat Tory interest.[44]

It was in 1777, after Etherington became bankrupt, that the paper was published by Blanchard as the *York Chronicle and General Advertiser*. Blanchard made a great success of the paper, and it is no surprise he was praised by the likes of William Hargrove, the local writer who described him as 'a very respectable native of the city'.[45] Besides serving as Grand Secretary for the York Grand Lodge, Blanchard was chosen as a member of the York Corporation in February 1790 and served as Sheriff in 1817.[46] He became the last surviving member of the York Grand Lodge and was the custodian of their artefacts and minute books. Blanchard died in 1836, having managed the *York Chronicle* for

almost sixty years as editor and proprietor. After his death, the paper was published by Henry Bellerby, as the *York Chronicle and Northern Standard*, until it was bought by the owners of the *Yorkshire Gazette* in 1839.[47]

With booksellers and printing presses, York became a progressive centre for education and indeed, the promotion and celebration of York itself, something that can be seen in Drake's *Eboracum*. York was also a northern centre for natural philosophy, with John Marsden, who was Grand Master of the York Grand Lodge in 1734, advertising, at his residence in Stonegate, a '*Course of Chymistry*' in the *York Courant* in November 1729. It was an interest that resounded in the lives of other Freemasons at this time, such as that energetic exponent of Newtonian natural philosophy, Dr John Theophilus Desaguliers.[48] Among York's scientific community was John Goodricke (1764-86), a gifted mathematician, chemist and astronomer, the Goodricke family having had connections to some members of the early York 'Grand Lodge', and, like Drake, became a Fellow of the Royal Society.[49] Stonegate was thus a thriving intellectual centre of printing presses, booksellers and education, with local Freemasons and their circle being directly involved in writing works, printing newspapers and even the tutelage of local scientific courses.

## The Black Swan, Coney Street (now demolished)

There were many inns and taverns where the York Grand Lodge met during the eighteenth century, the Black Swan being one of the most famous. A tavern was an establishment that offered eating and drinking, an inn on the other hand offered accommodation, but both, depending on the size, could offer a private room for a lodge to meet and dine in privately. There are two plaques that mark the site of the Black Swan on Coney Street, which was a meeting place for the York brethren in 1725. The Black Swan was a renowned coaching inn, with a coaching service to London that, according to an advertisement from the period,

22

Apollo Lodge, such as Minster organist John Camidge.[51] The Apollo Lodge had also met on Coney Street at the George Inn when the lodge was founded in 1773, the founders of the lodge being ex-members of the York Grand Lodge.

Gentlemen's clubs and societies were an integral part of eighteenth century English society, and along with Freemasonry, formed part of the thriving intellectual scene of towns and cities such as York. For example, author of *Tristram Shandy*, Laurence Stern, was a member of the Demoniacks Club, which met at John Hall Stevenson's Skelton Castle in Yorkshire, renamed Crazy Castle.[52] Other leading societies included the York Agricultural Society, founded by the Scottish physician Dr Alexander Hunter FRS, who practised in York. These clubs provided a networking nexus for gentlemen; a brotherly bond that supplied business contacts and a consortium of like-minded characters.

took four days 'God willing'. The figure of the Black Swan itself, which stood above the doorway to the inn, can be found in the York Castle Museum. The site of the inn is currently a British Home Stores.[50]

## The Good Humour Club, Sunton's Coffee House, Coney Street

The Good Humour Club was a gentlemen's club that operated from c.1725-1800, which met at Sunton's Coffee House in Coney Street, York, the club merrily celebrating the twin virtues of companionship and conviviality - virtues that were not too dissimilar to the ones found in Freemasonry. The club, which was also known as the Doctor's Club (each member was given the honorary title of Doctor), was one of the many gentlemen's clubs that operated in York during the eighteenth century. It included many local Freemasons throughout its existence - both from the York Grand Lodge and lodges under the Moderns, Masons such as Robert Sinclair who served as Grand Master of the York Grand Lodge, and various members from the Modern

## The White Swan, Petergate (now demolished)

The York Grand Lodge was recorded as meeting here a number of times from 1724-1730. As with the Black Swan, during the time that the York brethren met here, the innkeeper was also a member of the lodge. According to Masonic historian Neville Barker Cryer in his *York Mysteries Revealed*, the parish constables kept watch on the White Swan for what was termed 'illegal activities of the Papists' in 1723. The fact that the York Grand Lodge began meeting there shortly after this may suggest that they were not inclined to worry about the reputation of the establishment too much, especially how some of their number were open Catholics and Jacobites.[53]

**The Old Star Inn, accessed from a passage off Stonegate (now demolished)**

The Old Star Inn was set in its own courtyard, hidden behind the main street, and could only be accessed via a side passage from Stonegate. It was a popular meeting place for the York Grand Lodge, the brethren meeting there 1 times between 1725-1729; its location perhaps offering an element of secrecy in itself. Again, the innkeeper at the time, Luke Lowther, was also a member of the lodge.[54]

**The Globe Inn, No. 25 The Shambles (now demolished)**

The York Grand Lodge or the Old York Lodge, as it was known before it adopted the 'Grand Lodge' title, met at the Globe Inn during Christmastide in 1721. The Shambles is perhaps one of the most beautiful sections of the ancient city, its medieval architecture and narrow streets almost taking the visitor back in time. The Globe Inn closed in 1936.[55]

**Davy Hall, Davygate (now demolished)**

The Old York Lodge also met at Davy Hall in 1724. Davy Hall was, as Barker Cryer mentions in his *York Mysteries*, one of York's greatest medieval mansions, but was sadly demolished in 1745 to create New Street.[56]

**Guy Fawkes Inn, 25 High Petergate**

The Guy Fawkes Inn is situated nearby to the Masonic Hall at Duncombe Place and stands in the shadow of the Minster. It is a regular watering hole for Masons who gather there for a quick drink before the lodge meeting. Guy Fawkes was a Catholic who was involved in the failed Gunpowder Plot of 1605 and, though not a Mason (the first recorded English Freemason being Elias Ashmole in 1646), he was born on the site of the inn in 1570 and was baptised in the church opposite. He was also educated in York, and this traditionally styled inn celebrates his connection with York.

Yorkshire had acted as a northern hotbed for Catholic sympathisers, with some of the leading gentry adhering to the old religion. After the Dissolution of the Monasteries by Henry VIII, Catholics from Yorkshire took part in the Pilgrimage of Grace, an uprising against Henry's religious reforms. Many leading Yorkshire families, such as the Palmes family, remained openly Catholic; brothers George and John Palmes, who both served as Grand Masters of the York Grand Lodge, and Sir Thomas Gascoigne, who also served as Grand Master of York, were all Catholics. The rebellious spirit of the York Grand Lodge certainly reflected the similar feeling of the leading Catholic families of Yorkshire, and indeed, resounded the simmering rivalry between York and London.

# THE MERCHANT ADVENTURERS' HALL, THE GUILDHALL AND THE MERCHANT TAYLORS HALL

The York Mercers constructed this beautiful and atmospheric timber-framed medieval building in 1357 and it was only later in the fifteenth century that it became the Merchant Adventurers. It was in the hall where the management and planning of the export of cloth took place from the fifteenth to the seventeenth centuries, but by the early eighteenth century, the local York Freemasons began to meet there. The hall was the location for a meeting of York Masons on the Festival of St, John the Evangelist

*Merchants Adventurers' Hall.*

on 27 December 1725, where Charles Bathurst Esq. was chosen as Grand Master – the first time the title had been used by York.[57]

The following year, the York Masons met at the hall once again, this particular meeting being the event for Dr Francis Drake's famous speech. This again took place on the Feast of St. John the Evangelist, on 27 December 1726, and, for the first time, the use of the term Grand Lodge was used. In the speech, Drake outlined the claims of the York Grand Lodge: '...we can boast that the first Grand Lodge ever held in England, was held in this City; where Edwin, the first Christian King of the Northumbers,

about the Six Hundredth Year after Christ, and laid the Foundation of our Cathedral, sat as Grand Master.' Drake also highlighted hints of the rivalry with London, saying 'we are content they enjoy the Title of Grand Master of England; but the Totius Angliae we claim as our undoubted Right'.[58]

The speech, or oration as it is widely referred to, is indeed the earliest preserved Masonic speech,[59] and it is vitally important not just for Masonic historians, but for social historians as well. The speech became very popular amongst Masons of York, Antient and Modern persuasions during the eighteenth century, and printed many times; first in 1727, possibly for the York Masons themselves, then an expanded edition was published in London in 1729. This included an oration by the renowned London Grand Lodge Mason Edward Oakley, and an account of a Drury Lane performance of Shakespeare's *Henry IV* included as an added extra. This expanded version saw a second edition, published again in London, in 1734. The speech also found its way into Cole's *Constitutions* in 1729, becoming somewhat of an essential Masonic text, and obviously popular with both York and London Masons alike.[60]

In the same speech, Drake addressed his audience: 'To You, my Brethren, the Working Masons...To You, that are of other Trades and Occupations, and have the Honour to be admitted into this Society...And now, Gentlemen, I have reserv'd my last Admonitions for You...', indicating a social mixture of both 'operative' and 'speculative' Freemasons.[61] The Hall was also the meeting place for the Apollo Lodge, which was a local lodge under the 'Moderns' and met there during the later eighteenth century, meeting there for the first time on 7 November 1781. This particular meeting incidentally also included the organist for the York Minster, John Camidge, as Master.[62] The Apollo Lodge met at the hall throughout the 1780s, regularly celebrating the feasts of St John the Baptist's day, normally on or around 24 June, and St John the Evangelist's day, normally on or around 27 December. In the nineteenth century, the York 'Union' Lodge also met at the Merchant Adventurers' Hall, meeting there from 1848 to 1854, after which the lodge moved to the Masonic Hall at Blake Street.[63] The Merchant Adventurers' Hall is now a museum and is also open for events, and can be found on Fossgate. As one of York's most beautiful medieval buildings, along with its unique Masonic history, it is well worth a visit.

## The Guildhall

The current Guildhall was rebuilt after bombing damage during World War II, but it was rebuilt in keeping with the original gothic style of the old fifteenth century building. The building was the meeting place of York's Guilds, who controlled the trade and the quality of the craftsmanship of the city. The original walls on the whole survived the raid and still display mason's marks.

## The Merchant Taylors Hall

There is also the Merchant Taylors Hall, which also dates from the fifteenth century, the tailors being mentioned in the Freeman's Rolls as early as 1273. These halls were used for meetings and to celebrate feast days, the tailors being strongly connected with the religious and charitable confraternity of St John the Baptist.[64] The Guilds also took part in the York Mystery Plays, which became part of the celebration of the festival of Corpus Christi from the fourteenth century, the cycle of plays re-enacting stories of the Bible from the Creation to the Last Judgement. A particular Guild would be responsible for part of the play, for example the masons would organise, finance and sometimes even perform the Coming of the Three Kings to Herod, the carpenters the Resurrection, and the tailors the Ascension.[65] The York Mystery Plays continued up until 1569, but have recently been revived.[66]

# MASONIC HALLS IN YORK

## Duncombe Place, Masonic Hall

Duncombe Place is the location of the Masonic Hall and is the home of the York Lodge; the custodians of the manuscripts and artefacts of the independent York Grand Lodge. The building is hidden somewhat, and is rather unimposing, but it holds Masonic secrets that would not only entice the Masonic researcher, but anyone with an interest in local or social history. The York Lodge No. 236 founded in 1777 as a Modern lodge, was originally called the Union Lodge, the lodge first meeting in Lockwood's Coffee House, before moving to the Theatre Coffee House in Top Lane, York, in 1786. One of the reasons given for the move was that the Tyler, who was the owner of Lockwood's Coffee House, was frequently absent from his post of guarding the outside door of the lodge, perhaps being tempted away by the business of his establishment. Another move to the Golden Lion Inn in Thursday Market ensued, followed by seven more moves; the lodge meeting in the Merchant Adventurers' Hall for a time and two of the moves being to Blake Street, a premises that stood on the same location of the present hall.[67]

In 1859, a special committee reported that they had agreed with the proprietors of the building in which the Provincial Masonic Lodge was housed 'for the purchase of the premises together with the front house in Little Blake Street for the sum of £550'. The building was then bought and adapted for the lodge. In 1861, the York Corporation Street Improvement Committee decided that the narrowness of the street was causing major problems and leading to congestion, and the newly purchase building was demolished. However, the lodge received

adequate compensation along with 293 square yards of land, giving the lodge an opportunity to construct a purpose built hall on the site.

The plans for the construction were commissioned and a member of the lodge; a certain Brother Oates, who was an architect, put forward his ideas, and a London based brother, J. Barton Wilson, drew up the drawings for the interior of the temple room. The foundation stone was laid at the north-east corner of what would become the lodge room on 8 September 1862, along with a jar filed with relics, and on 2 June the following year, an 'extraordinary lodge' was called for the purpose of opening and consecrating the new hall. However, the lodge membership had grown quickly and in 1866, yet another committee was formed to assess expansion of the building, and it was suggested a year later that the front elevation should be taken down and extended 12 feet, creating a larger dining area upstairs. In doing so, the hall lost its original '2nd degree' winding staircase to create a larger foyer, and its original Doric porch (the location of which can still be seen by the outline of the fresher stone projecting from the library wall).[68]

The hall that exists today includes an excellent library and archive that is surely the northern rival of London; it includes all the surviving rolls and minute books of the York Grand Lodge, the constitution rolls, the earliest of which dates from c.1600, the York Grand Lodge board, and many ceramics, jewels, and other rare and valuable Masonic objects. Upstairs in the dining room, which elegantly overlooks the Minster, prints of past York Grand Masters hang on the wall, watching the diners as they toast current Grand officers, and a banner

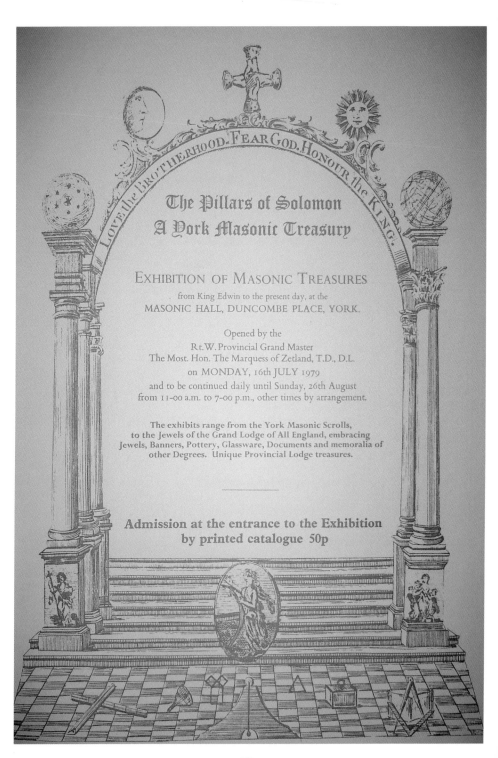

**The Pillars of Solomon**
**A York Masonic Treasury**

EXHIBITION OF MASONIC TREASURES
from King Edwin to the present day, at the
MASONIC HALL, DUNCOMBE PLACE, YORK.

Opened by the
Rt.W. Provincial Grand Master
The Most. Hon. The Marquess of Zetland, T.D., D.L.
on MONDAY, 16th JULY 1979
and to be continued daily until Sunday, 26th August
from 11-00 a.m. to 7-00 p.m., other times by arrangement.

The exhibits range from the York Masonic Scrolls,
to the Jewels of the Grand Lodge of All England, embracing
Jewels, Banners, Pottery, Glassware, Documents and memoralia of
other Degrees. Unique Provincial Lodge treasures.

**Admission at the entrance to the Exhibition**
**by printed catalogue 50p**

LOVE the BROTHERHOOD. FEAR GOD. HONOUR the KING.

*Cover of the catalogue for the Exhibition of Masonic Treasures at Duncombe Place.*

can be seen that was carried by the York 'Union' Lodge during a procession to mark the funeral of Admiral Lord Nelson.

The temple or lodge room is full of Masonic history; the lodge furniture being an eclectic mix of furniture from the York Grand Lodge and the Modern lodge, creating a unique working lodge room with artefacts still being used. The last surviving member of the York Grand Lodge – the last Grand Secretary William Blanchard, presented the items to the York 'Union' Lodge, after the demise of the Grand Lodge, and they were incorporated into the working lodge; for example the 'Obligating Pedestal', originally presented to the York Grand Lodge by Sir Thomas Gascoigne in 1771 when he was installed as Grand Master is still in use, the three mahogany and silver candlesticks are still used, and the York Grand Lodge banner. The hall is ready to give up its many secrets, and the following artefacts, rolls and manuscripts are just some of the many mysteries held at Duncombe Place.[69]

### The York Grand Lodge Board

Of all the artefacts that once belonged to the York Grand Lodge, the board is the most revealing in respect of the symbolism that was used, especially with the modern use of tracing boards in the Craft degrees under the UGLE. Artist and Arms painter Thomas Beckwith painted the board, which displays pyramids, rainbows and reveals the Crypt of the York Minster. Thomas settled into the York Grand Lodge with ease; he was made an Entered Apprentice and Fellow Craft in the York Grand Lodge on the same day on 31 March 1777 and

was made a Master Mason later in the same year on 24 November. He was appointed Junior Grand Warden by 1778, and served as Senior Grand Warden for the year 1780. The board is now in possession of the York 'Union' Lodge No. 236 and hangs in the lodge room, the lodge also having an engraving of his self-portrait. Thomas was also a passionate local historian and genealogist; he collected pedigrees of Yorkshire gentry and compiled Arms and crests of families, a collection of which can now be found in the Yorkshire Archaeological Society.[70]

There were a number of Beckwiths who were members of the York Grand Lodge. It is hard to establish if they were all related, but as in the case with the York Grand Lodge, many members of localised extended families were involved throughout its existence. One such gentleman, Josiah Beckwith of Rotherham, has been referred to as the brother of Thomas by York Grand Lodge historians Whytehead and G. Y. Johnson.[71] Indeed, 'Bror Beckwith' proposed Josiah, who was an Attorney, on 8 December 1777. After being made an Entered Apprentice and Fellow Craft on a meeting held on 20

*The York Grand Lodge board painted by Thomas Beckwith.* (Courtesy of the York Lodge library, Duncombe Place)

29

March 1778, 'Bror. Thos. Beckwith proposed Brors. Josiah Beckwith & Thos. Alderson to be Raisd to the degree of M.Ms' on 27 April.[72] So Thomas did have a hand at proposing Josiah, and worked with him for the petition for constituting a new lodge in Rotherham called the Druidical Lodge, the petition presented at a York Grand Lodge meeting on 12 October 1778.[73] Josiah Beckwith was elected as a Fellow of the Society of Antiquaries in 1777, and in 1784, he published a revised edition of Blount's *Ancient Tenures & Jocular Customs of Manors*, which became a much celebrated work in antiquarian circles. He also had an extensive library, which was sold after he became bankrupt. He had moved to London and died there in 1791.[74]

**York MS No.1**

The earliest possible reference to non-operative or speculative Freemasons in Yorkshire was mentioned by Masonic historian Neville Barker Cryer in his book *York Mysteries Revealed*, in which he identified two men who were named in an introduction to a version of the 'Old Charges' written on a manuscript entitled the York MS No. 1, dated to c.1600. The introduction reads:

*An Anagraime upon the name of Masonrie*
*William Kay to his friend Robt Preston*
*Upon his Artt of Masonrie as Followeth:*[75]

Barker Cryer put forward that the two men mentioned in the document were local Freemen from York; William Kay who was accepted as a spurrier in 1569, and Robert Preston who was accepted as a fishmonger in 1571, suggesting that they were at least interested in and involved with 'Masonrie'.[76] The manuscript is certainly a very important and intriguing document, especially when analysing the wording of the anagram which states 'Upon his Artt of Masonrie', suggesting that the Robert Preston mentioned in the manuscript was certainly interested in the 'Artt' in some form. Michael Baigent however, who wrote the rather sensationalist foreword to Barker Cryer's book, was less cautious and

erroneously stated that these men had actually joined a lodge in York, when there is no actual mention of them being in a York based lodge at all.[77] These two men were connected with each other in some way, to appear at the beginning of the document. However, the precise nature of their involvement with 'Masonrie' remains a mystery, as there is no other supporting evidence. They were certainly involved in the writing of these 'Old Charges', perhaps in a similar way that the 'Old Charges' written for the lodge in Warrington mentioned by Elias Ashmole in 1646, was compiled by Edward Sankey, son of lodge member Richard Sankey.[78]

Moreover, according to a written inscription on the reverse of the manuscript, Dr Francis Drake only presented the York MS No.1 to the York Grand Lodge in 1736. It states it had been found during the demolition of Pontefract Castle, which occurred after its surrender as a Royalist stronghold at the end of the second stage of the Civil War in 1649.[79] Drake's grandfather, before being ordained as a vicar, was a Royalist officer and was present during the siege, so Dr Francis Drake's family could have previously kept the manuscript.[80] Godfrey Higgins also mentions that the manuscript was taken to the castle for safe keeping during the Civil War. The York MS No.1 is certainly an enigmatic document, and there are more artefacts and manuscripts that give an insight into the 'Artt of Masonrie' in Yorkshire.

**The Mahogany Flat Rule**

Another important artefact held at Duncombe Place which refers to seventeenth century non-operative Freemasonry, is the mahogany flat rule with a date of 1663, measuring 18 inches, now held by the York 'Union' Lodge, displaying Masonic symbols and mentioning three men associated with York:

| Iohn Drake | William | ✿ | Baron: 1663 |
| | of Yorke | | Iohn ✿ Baron |

30

John Drake seems to have been collated to the Prebendal Stall of Donnington in the Cathedral Church of York in October 1663, and was a cousin of Dr Francis Drake's father; William Baron was made a Freeman grocer in 1662, serving as sheriff of York in 1677, and

*The York MS No. 1 revealing the anagram. The manuscript itself dates to c.1600.*
(Courtesy of the York Lodge library, Duncombe Place)

John Baron may have been a relative of his.[81] Again, no lodge mentioned, but the evidence of the rule, the symbols, and the mention of a member of the Drake family and of a prominent Freeman of York is suggestive of a locally important gathering, which certainly used the 'Artt of Masonrie'.

## The York MS No.4

Thirty years after the date shown on the mahogany flat rule, a parchment roll dated to 1693 entitled the York MS No.4 - another copy of the 'Old Charges' - mentions six men who were members of a lodge in Yorkshire.[82] This version of the 'Old Charges' was written by a certain Mark Kypling, who, along with the other men named, have been associated with the Tees Valley in the North Riding.[83] It is indeed a very interesting version as it mentions at the start of the ceremony of making a Mason, 'that hee or shee that is to be made Mason', being an early and extremely rare example of a woman being able to enter into the Craft.[84] Writing about the York MS No.4, the nineteenth century Masonic historian W. J. Hughan stated that 'we believe it likely that women were admitted as members of the old masonic Guilds, (when their husbands or fathers were deceased) if they were in a position to carry on their Trade'. He went on to say that:

"[the] Apprentice Charge" considered to be peculiar to this MS. has since been discovered in the "Harlelan 1942" and the "Hope" MSS. Evidently the Apprentices were required according to this charge, (which was composed of ten clauses), to serve their Master or Dame, as the case may be ; thus there is pidma facie, evidence of females occupying the position of Employers, and therefore it is probable they were in some respects accounted members of the Masonic Body'.[85]

Despite this version of the 'Old Charges' clearly mentioning that women could be made a Mason, there is no evidence of women joining lodges in York, and the York MS No.4 was only presented to the York Grand Lodge in 1777, by Brother George Walker of Wetherby.[86] There is however, the intriguing case of a woman entering a lodge in Cork, Ireland, a short time after the York MS No.4 was written.

In an exposé of the later eighteenth century called Jachin and Boaz, there is an interesting mention of a lodge in Ireland that admitted a woman, the anonymous author of the work stating that she was 'as good a Mason as any of them'.[87] This Lady Freemason is named as the Hon. Elizabeth Aldworth, born in 1693, the daughter of Arthur St. Leger, first Viscount Doneraile, who was said to have held a lodge in his home at Doneraile Court, County Cork. According to the Memoir of the Lady Freemason, it was at one of these lodge meetings that Elizabeth overheard the activities of the lodge while reading in the library room next door. Some of the bricks from the dividing wall between the library and the room where the lodge was meeting could be removed, so Elizabeth was able to watch the lodge proceedings through the narrow gap. After watching the ceremony, Elizabeth then tried to leave the library be leaving through a door that would lead through the far end of the room where the lodge was held. However, she was confronted by her father's butler who was acting as Tyler, and after raising an alarm, she was 'detained' in the library. The Brethren of the lodge then discussed what best to do; their secrets had been revealed, so a decision was made to make Elizabeth a Freemason. As there are no lodge records, the date of her initiation has been placed between 1710-1712.[88] The York MS No.4 is thus an important manuscript for revealing this aspect of early Freemasonry, and is an informative and valuable example of the 'Old Charges' collection.

## The York MS No.7

As we have already seen, the York Grand Lodge only referred to itself as having a Grand Master in 1725 and as the actual 'Grand Lodge of all England' the following year, a shift that suggests a reaction against the London based 'Premier/Modern' Grand Lodge. Despite this, Gould in his History of Freemasonry suggested that it had its actual foundations much earlier, giving a date of 1705 in which a 'governing body' at York began. Indeed, the list of the 'Presidents' of this governing body begins in 1705 and their role was much like that of Grand Master. From 1712, we have the minutes of this Old Lodge at York displayed in a manuscript entitled the York MS No.7. This supplies the earliest positive evidence that lodge meetings were held intermittently throughout the year at various local inns; such as Luke Lowther's Star Inn in Stonegate and John Colling's White Swan in Petergate, both of the proprietors being members of the York Lodge.[89] These lodge meetings were, on the whole, termed as 'private lodges', but were occasionally called 'General lodges' such as the one held at the house of James Boreham in Stonegate on St John's Day on 24 June 1713, or at certain times during the Christmas period as 'St John's lodges', such as in 1716 and 1721.[90] By the time we come to 27 December 1725, the term 'Grand Feast' was used for the first time after a procession to the Merchant's Adventurers' Hall, and the following year, the title of Grand Lodge was used for the first time.[91] The minutes end on 4 May 1730, this manuscript being a valuable insight into how the Old York Lodge evolved into that of a Grand Lodge.

Duncombe Place is not open to the public, but a visit can be arranged by contacting the York Lodge via their website.[92] There are other lodges based in York, and they meet in York's other Masonic Hall which is situated in Castlegate.

## Castlegate House, Castlegate

Castlegate House is the location for the second Masonic temple in York, and is home to York's other lodges, such as the Francis Drake Lodge No.7825, which was founded in 1962, and named after the illustrious Grand Master of the York Grand Lodge.[93] Castlegate House is a beautiful Georgian town house completed in 1763 and, like Fairfax House, which is just opposite, was designed by John Carr.[94] Castlegate House has a Masonic temple extension, which dates from 1920, and is also the location for a number of other lodges and side Orders, such as Alcuin Lodge No.6300, which was founded in 1946, and is the 'University lodge' of York; having a dispensation to accept men as members from the age of 18.[95] Another lodge, which meets at Castlegate House, is Agricola Lodge No.1991, founded in 1883, being named quite aptly after a Roman General, as the lodge was originally a military lodge.[96] Like Duncombe Place, Castlegate House is not open to the public, but a visit can be arranged by contacting the lodges that meet there.

*The Masonic Hall, Castlegate House.*

# CIVIC BUILDINGS ASSOCIATED WITH YORK FREEMASONS

**Fairfax House, No.27 Castlegate** – *residence of the Fairfax family, a member of whom was Admiral Robert Fairfax, Deputy President of the York Grand Lodge*

Admiral Robert Fairfax, was 'admitted and sworn into the honourable Society and fraternity of Freemasons' on 7 August 1713, and was the Deputy President mentioned in the York minutes for December 1721. He was born in February 1665/6, the second son of William Fairfax of Steeton and Newton Kyme in Yorkshire, England, and the grandson of Sir William Fairfax. He was commissioned to Vice-Admiral of the Blue in January 1708, but the commission was cancelled and given to another officer who was favoured over him for political reasons. Fairfax was subsequently made a Rear admiral and a Lord of the Admiralty, but he retired from the Navy in the October. He then entered politics and at a by-election in 1713, he was returned to Parliament for the city of York, but lost his seat in the general election after the accession of George I. Fairfax had in the meantime, been elected as Alderman of York, and elected Lord Mayor in 1715. He died on 17 October 1725.

The house itself was built in the 1740s, and was redesigned by John Carr in the 1760s for Charles Gregory Fairfax, the 9th Viscount Fairfax of Emley. The house has been described as one of the most beautiful Georgian townhouses in York, and though it was built after Robert's death, there is an interesting portrait of Admiral Fairfax holding a compass, though this is symbolic of his position as Lord of the Admiralty.[97] Viscount Fairfax was a Catholic, and the house is adorned with

imagery that can be interpreted as Jacobite symbolism, such as the rosebuds that feature on the staircase balustrade, the imagery of the rosebuds during the eighteenth century being a widely used Jacobite symbol. The oak leaf sprig displayed on a wall panel by the main staircase can also be interpreted as a Jacobite symbol.[98] John Carr was the son of a master mason, and being born in Yorkshire, was arguably the leading architect in the north of England during the eighteenth century, designing many buildings in the Palladian style. Carr also designed other buildings in York such as the County Lunatic Asylum and the Assize Courts, and his prominence in the city can be reflected in him serving as Lord Mayor of York in 1770 and again in 1785. Despite Carr being the son of a master mason and his position as the local leading architect, he was not a member of the York Grand Lodge.[99]

**The Assembly Rooms**

Lord Burlington, friend and benefactor of York Grand Lodge Mason Dr Francis Drake, designed the Assembly Rooms at York based on the *Egyptian Hall* of Vitruvius, as interpreted by Palladio; the rooms symbolising and celebrating the ancient classical Roman architecture of York. Though no record exists of Lord Burlington as a Freemason, he was listed in Anderson's *Constitutions* as "displaying the Art", and his circle, which included the architects William Kent and Colen Campbell, was responsible for numerous publications on the architectural designs of Palladio and Inigo Jones. Whether Burlington was or was not a Freemason, he certainly knew many, including the poet Alexander Pope, and architect, Nicholas Hawksmoor. He socialised with Grand Masters, such as the second Duke of Montagu, and discussed Roman architecture with later York Grand Master Francis Drake, and perhaps as a non-Mason, Burlington held no prejudices in regards to London or York Freemasons. Even one of Burlington's draughtsmen, Samuel Savill, belonged to a lodge that met at the Cock and Bottle, in London's Little Britain.[100]

Drake was a notorious Jacobite, and it has been suggested, despite only circumstantial evidence, that Burlington may himself have been a secret Jacobite; Burlington incorporating Jacobite symbolism into his designs and the decoration of his home Chiswick Villa. If true, Burlington's Jacobite leanings would have especially bonded him to Drake in a deeper political sense, in addition to their shared interest in architecture.[101] Burlington's Chiswick Villa in London has at least two rooms that clearly reflect Masonic symbolism, the Red and Blue Velvet Rooms. Both reveal

an array of distinctive Masonic symbols and have their ceilings adorned with representations of the heavens. The Blue Velvet Room in particular, focuses on divine architecture, actually displaying 'architecture' as a goddess residing in the heavens, holding the compasses, accompanied by three cherubs, each holding Masonic tools. The goddess is also holding what appears to be a variation on the plan of the Temple of Fortuna Virilis after Palladio, and is similar to Villalpando's reconstruction of the inner sanctum of the Temple; Burlington having his three-volume works in his library inventory. The room's measurements resonate Masonic influence, being 15 x 15 x 15 feet, a perfect cube, reflecting perfect architecture, and again having similar proportions to Villalpando's and Newton's versions of Solomon's Temple. The actual design of the Chiswick House was inspired by Palladio's Villa Rotonda near Vicenza, the square plan and layout not only bearing a remarkable resemblance to Villalpando's plan of the inner sanctum of Solomon's Temple, but also

*The architectural splendour of the Assembly Rooms designed by Lord Burlington, the earliest Palladian buildings in the north of England. The building became a focal point for the social elite of York.* Photo (https://commons.wikimedia.org/wiki/File:Ask_at_the_Assembly_Rooms,_Blake_Street,_York_ (21st _October_2010).jpg by Mtaylor848 / CC BY (https://creativecommons.org/licenses/by-sa/3.0/deed.en)

| Year | N°. | Names of the Brethren | made E.A.'s and F.C.'s | Raised M.M.'s |
|------|-----|-----------------------|------------------------|---------------|
| 1770 | 87 | Thomas Johnson | 10th Dec: | 10th Dec: 1770 |
| | 88 | Charles Varley | Ditto | Ditto |
| | 89 | Taylor | Ditto | Ditto |
| | 90 | William Arnold | Ditto | Ditto |
| 1771 | 91 | Charles Turner Esq | 14 Jan.y | |
| | 92 | George Kittson | Ditto | 25 march |
| | 93 | Thomas Powell | 28 Jan.y | 8. April |
| | 94 | Jude Webster | 11th Feb | 11. March |
| | 95 | Tate Wilkinson | F.C. 11 Feb | 8. April |
| | 96 | Joseph Reynoldson | 11th Feb: | 25. March |
| | 97 | James Wiggins | 25 Feb: | 25. March |
| | 99 | Rich.d Peel | Ditto | |
| | 100 | James Wiggins of Leeds | 25 march | 8. April |
| | 101 | Thomas Thackray | 25 Feb: | 11 March |
| | 102 | George Walker of Leeds | 8th April | 27 Apr. 1772 |
| | 103 | Richard Walker of Wetherby | 8 April | 13 May |
| | 104 | John Taylor | 12 Aug.st | 9 Sept: |
| | 105 | Robert Wallis | 9 Sept.r | 9 Decm.r |
| | 106 | John Prince | 23 Dec.r | |
| | 107 | William Edmonds | Ditto | 30 march 1772 |
| 1772 | 108 | Walter Hawksworth | | 23 Dec: |
| | 109 | John Playter | 10th Feb: | 30 March |
| | 110 | Stephen Jager | 24 Feb: | |
| | 111 | John Thorney | 27 Jan: | 30 March |
| | 112 | Robert Haxby | 23 May | 28 Sept |
| | 113 | John Cordley | 30 Nov: | 25 Jan 1773 |
| | 114 | Rich.d Garland | Ditto | Ditto |

*A list of York Grand Lodge Masons. Almost all on the page appear to have undergone their initiation and passing during one day, being raised to a Master Mason on another. An exception to this was theatre manager Tate Wilkinson, who is specifically entered on the list as becoming a Fellow Craft.*

representing a set of proportions, which fuelled Burlington's taste in classical architecture.[102]

Burlington had witnessed first-hand the classical architecture of Italy during his Grand Tour, and quickly became what was termed the 'High Priest of Palladianism'. He had studied in depth the divine measurements as used by Palladio, incorporating meticulously the measurements used in Palladio's Rotonda, in his design of the villa. The Rotonda was Palladio's ideal villa, and best represents the relationship between Palladio and the Ancients. Here, Solomon's Temple was considered the ultimate source for the Greek and Roman orders, with Villalpando describing it as an embodiment of classical harmony that God had disclosed to Solomon. This harmony was thought to be the form of musical harmony, which both Pythagoras and Plato had discovered, a belief, which Villalpando disclosed in his writings. Burlington knew of the power of architecture; that the classical design captured the essence of Solomon's Temple, and as a result, was thought to possess the word of God, the Grand architect of the Universe.[103] Portraits of both Burlington and Drake can be seen displayed in the York Mansion House.

## The Theatre Royal

During its revival phase after 1761, the York Grand Lodge had a number of actors and 'strollers' as members, and one of the leading actors was Tate Wilkinson. Wilkinson, who according to Masonic historian Barker Cryer, became a member of the York Grand Lodge by at least 1770,[104] but was listed as a Fellow Craft in the York Grand Lodge register in February 1771, was an actor and manager of the Yorkshire circuit theatres, operating in York, Leeds, Hull and Doncaster. He was central to the theatrical scene of Yorkshire during the latter half of the eighteenth century, and worked with some of the most notable and talented actors of the period outside of London. Bridge Frodsham, a leading member of the York Punch Bowl Lodge, was perhaps the most renowned and talented stroller, being 'esteemed in York as a Garrick',

and was said to have even lectured David Garrick about Shakespeare.[105] Tate knew Frodsham very well, and commented on him, and a number of his fellow actors from the Punch Bowl Lodge, in his *Memoirs*.

The actors and comedians of the eighteenth century would certainly have been attracted to Freemasonry; the lodge room providing a perfect theatre for performing the ritual and the social aspect of Masonry supplying contacts. Indeed, Frodsham's famous 'charge' which was subsequently published, gives an element of the dramatic rhetoric that he was renowned for, the language used providing a hint of how the Punch Bowl Lodge would have operated. The 'charge' also seemed to touch on the friction between Modern and 'York' Masonry; putting forward that, 'in the north, when I see it, notwithstanding the virulence of its foes, rising to its primeval state; it immediately occurs to me, that the institution came from Heaven itself...'[106] The fact that York could attract such highly esteemed actors is certainly a testament to its cultural importance. The vital work done by Tate Wilkinson for the theatre in York can never be underestimated; in 1769 he paid £500 for a Royal Patent for the theatre, renaming it the Theatre Royal, and his company became renowned as the leading provincial company in England. Wilkinson left the York Grand Lodge in 1775. The building itself is a beautiful example of Georgian architecture; York being the location of some of the finest Georgian buildings in England.

## The Yorkshire Museum

Continued interest in natural philosophy in York can be seen with the formation of the Yorkshire Philosophical Society in 1822, which included a number of Freemasons – the most prominent member being Thomas Dundas MP. The Philosophical Society was behind the building of the Museum in 1829 and was active in saving a number of historic York buildings from demolition, such as part of the city walls.[107] The Yorkshire Philosophical Society became extremely popular, attracting the leading members of the Yorkshire intelligentsia, and a home was soon needed for the many archaeological, zoological and botanical collections that the members had donated, as well as the growing library of the Society. Donations for the Museum building fund not only came from the members, but from leading figures in Yorkshire society, some of whom were also prominent Freemasons or linked to Freemasonry, such as Robert Sinclair, Recorder of York and past Grand Master of the York Grand Lodge, who donated £20. Edward T. Copley (Wolley), the son of the last Grand Master of the York Grand Lodge, also gave £20, and Godfrey Higgins, author and Freemason, gave a donation of £25.[108] Other contributors to the Museum building fund included Richard Dalton of the York 'Union' Lodge, and many other recognisable names related to York Masons, such as Drake, Fairfax and Gascoigne.[109] Indeed, Higgins and Sinclair are an example of the many Freemasons at this time that supported the building of new civic buildings like the Museum: buildings that promoted education for the people and symbolise the charitable ethos of Masonry. Similar support for educational civic buildings can be seen in Warrington, Lancashire, where leading Freemasons were involved in many learned societies and actively took part in the laying of the foundation stone of the Warrington Museum and Library in 1855. Parallels can also be seen in other northern English towns such as Oldham, where local Masons supported the Oldham Lyceum and in Wigan, where the family of prominent Freemason Lord Lindsay actively supported the Mining and Mechanical School.[110] Godfrey Higgins was a keen archaeologist and was very much interested in Druidry, and certainly exemplifies the interests of certain Freemasons who put forward ideas on the romantic origins of Masonry at this time, displayed in the works of Thomas Paine and Richard Carlile for example, capturing the public imagination and at the same time, promoting Masonry as a Society with a more ancient past.[111]

The Yorkshire Museum building itself, is designed in a Greek Revival Style by celebrated architect William Wilkins (who incidentally had previously designed a Freemasons' Hall in Bath), and was officially opened in 1830 – being one of the longest established museums in the country. A botanical garden was added and an observatory, which now houses the astronomy collection. The museum became a celebrated centre for the promotion of science, and in 1831 was the scene for the inaugural meeting of the British Association for the Advancement of Science.

*The Yorkshire Museum was founded by the Yorkshire Philosophical Society to house their collection, and was built in the Greek Revival Style and opened in 1830. Many local Freemasons gave donations for the building, such as Godfrey Higgins and Robert Sinclair.* Photo (https://commons.wikimedia.org/wiki/File:Yorkshire_Museum.jpg) by Kaly99 / CC BY (https://creativecommons.org/licenses/by-sa/3.0/deed.en

# THE MINSTER AND OTHER CHURCHES IN AND AROUND YORK ASSOCIATED WITH FREEMASONS

## St. Helen's Church

St. Helen's Church in Stonegate is a medieval church that is connected to the final years of the York Grand Lodge through The Rev. John Parker, who was the 'Grand Chaplain' of the York Grand Lodge. After the demise of the Grand Lodge, he visited the Modern York 'Union' Lodge a total of 25 times between 1802 and 1814, and he was regularly referred to in the minutes as the 'Grand Chaplain'.[112] The Rev. Parker seemed to have especially endeared himself to the 'Union' Lodge, first appearing at a Lodge of Emergency where he conducted the ceremony for the burial of a Brother Dunn on 10 March 1802.[113] The Reverend was duly thanked by the lodge in a letter, and during a meeting on 1 June that year for 'The Thanksgiving for the Blessings of Peace', he accompanied the lodge on a procession, giving a much thanked discourse and was later joined by fellow York Grand Lodge member Robert Sinclair.[114] On 27 August 1802, The Rev. Parker and the last Grand Master of the York Grand Lodge Edward Wolley both visited the 'Union' Lodge together, both being referred to in the present tense as members of the Grand Lodge of All England, which may hint that, at the very least, they considered themselves as still being members.[115]

The Rev. Parker continued to visit quite regularly, seemingly being adopted by the local Modern Lodge. The Reverend invited to preach appropriate sermons at St. Helen's Church after processions by the lodge, such as the one proposed by the Master on the interment of Lord Nelson on 16 December 1805, and the procession on 7 July 1814, to celebrate the peace following the Napoleonic War. Parker's death and burial in the June of 1815, at the age of 74, was much lamented and was mentioned in the *York Courant*. The good Reverend was referred to as, 'being Grand Chaplain in the Grand Lodge of all England, to the Provincial Grand Lodge of York, and the Apollo and Union Lodges', and that 'several of the fraternity were present.'[116] Parker had also evidently endeared himself to the York based Apollo Lodge, having conducted the burial service for the ex-York Grand Secretary John Browne while Brethren of the Apollo Lodge had attended and taken part in the ceremony.[117]

## St Mary's, Beverley

This beautiful medieval church is the final resting place of York Grand Master Dr Francis Drake. Drake had been the Grand Master in 1761-2 after its revival, however, by 1767, with his health failing, he left York to live with his eldest son, Francis, who was the vicar of St Mary's Church in Beverley. He died there on 16 March 1771 and was buried in the church, where his son placed a memorial tablet. Despite his high Office as Past Grand Master of the York Grand Lodge, there are no Masonic symbols or references on the memorial, and no mention of his burial in the York Grand Lodge minutes. The church itself began in the twelfth century, but most of the work dates from the fourteenth and fifteenth centuries. Drake's memorial tablet, the original in Latin and an English translation can be seen in the church.

## York Minster

The Minster probably has more Masonic symbols on display than any other building in

TRANSLATION
of INSCRIPTION
• • •

SACRED TO THE MEMORY OF
FRANCIS DRAKE
ESQUIRE
FELLOW OF THE ROYAL SOCIETY AND
ALSO OF [THE SOCIETY OF] ANTIQUARIES ·
HOW[EVER] MUCH HE PROGRESSED BY
HIS LEARNING AND APPLICATION, HIS
HISTORY OF YORK AND ALSO HIS
PARLIAMENTARY HISTORY CLEARLY
BEAR WITNESS · WHETHER SEEN AS A
FRIEND, A FELLOW-CITIZEN, OR A
COLLEAGUE, IN WHATEVER CIRCUMSTANCES
HE WAS IN, HE ATTRACTED THE GRATITUDE
AND LOVE OF EVERYONE TO AN ASTON-
ISHING DEGREE · SO KIND, SO
GENEROUS, SO COURTEOUS, HE
WAS NOT TO BE SURPASSED ·
FRANCIS DRAKE
DOCTOR OF DIVINITY,
HIS ELDEST SON AND VICAR OF THIS
CHURCH, SO WELL AWARE OF THE
MERITS OF HIS FATHER, WISHED
THIS MONUMENT TO BE MADE ·
HE DIED IN THE YEAR OF OUR LORD
1771 · AGED 76
• • •

NOTE - FRANCIS DRAKE (SENR) WAS BORN IN 1696 ·
HIS GRANDFATHER, FATHER, BROTHERS & SONS
WERE ALL CLERGYMEN · HE ALONE ELECTED
TO BECOME A DOCTOR... AND EVENTUALLY
YORK CITY SURGEON · AS AN HISTORIAN
HE ACHIEVED FAME · SPENDING HIS LAST
YEARS IN BEVERLEY, WITH HIS ELDEST
SON - VICAR OF THIS CHURCH - HE DIED
AND WAS BURIED HERE IN 1771 ·

*The transcription of the memorial stone of Dr Francis Drake at St. Mary's, Beverley.*

York; from the Mason's Loft, to the symbols displayed in the beautifully vivid stained glass windows and of course, the many stonemason's marks depicted on the magnificent medieval stonework. Christian activity at the site of the Minster dates back at least to Anglo-Saxon times, the chronicler Bede mentioning that King Edwin of the Northumbrians was baptized there in 627.[118] This was probably a wooden structure constructed on the site, but a stone building was completed at a later date. The church itself was built on the site of the old Roman headquarters of the city, and after being damaged during William the Conqueror's 'Harrying of the North' in 1069, rebuilding occurred and, around 1230, construction began on a glorious Gothic structure that was only finally completed in 1472.

Such extensive building work at York Minster during the medieval period demanded the long-term presence of operative stonemasons, and indeed, there are records of such masons, such as Master Mason William de Hoton, Jr., who was the draughtsman of the full size setting of an aisle window on the plaster floor of the York tracing house. William de Hoton had followed his father William de Hoton, Sr., as a Master Mason, both working on the building of the Minster during the fourteenth century. Other Master Masons are listed throughout the Gothic rebuilding phase of the Minster, such as Thomas de Pakenham in the 1340s and William Hyndeley at the end of the fifteenth century. These all appear in the York Minster Fabric Rolls, the rolls revealing an account of the expenses paid during the building work at the Minster.

Certain rolls also give a unique insight into the hierarchal structure and the rules of the operative masons, such as when:

'the principal and second masons, who are called

their masters, and the carpenter...who have been received by the Chapter, and will be received in perpetuity, shall swear in the presence of the Chapter, that they shall perform the ancient customs written below by means of the other masons, carpenters and other workmen, and they shall be faithfully observed...'[119]

The masons would thus go to the Chapter and swear to observe rules to ensure punctuality, order and the finest workmanship.[120] As early as 1349, a mason's lodge is mentioned in relation to the building of the Minster; the lodge being a workshop where the masons could cut and dress the stone for use in constructing the building.[121] This lodge would also be a place where the masons could eat, drink and rest, and they could discuss and plan their work; in 1349 for example, the records of the Minster list the tools of the lodge; a 'magna kevell' is recorded, along with 'mallietes', 'chisielles', a 'compas' and 'tracyngbordes'.[122] The use of aprons and

*The Minster.*

gloves are also mentioned in the Rolls, with 'setters' John Taillor and John Bultflow being given money for two skins from which to make aprons and 18d for ten pairs of gloves.[123]

Despite the completed structure of the Minster being consecrated in 1472, work continued for a number of years on the fabric, with Master Mason William Hyndeley for example designing a rood screen. Other buildings around York also demanded operative masons, such as the Bedern - part of the College of the Vicars Choral - which was completed in the fourteenth century, and of course the city walls, the castle and the many other medieval churches within York, all requiring both building and maintenance work by skilled stonemasons.

It was within this culture of civic building in York that certain masons took on important roles in the service of their community, such as Robert Couper who was admitted a freeman in 1443 and then appointed Chief Mason to the Corporation. He was also the leading mason in the building of the Guildhall. It is clear that masons were essential to the medieval

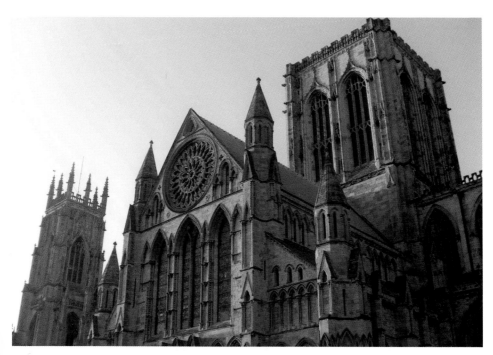

development of York, and even when we reach the Tudor period, these craftsmen were still serving important offices for the community, such as carver Thomas Drawswerd, who became a freeman in 1496, Chamberlain in 1501, Sheriff in 1505, alderman in 1508, MP for York in 1512, and Lord Mayor in 1515 and also in 1523.[124]

Between 1558 and 1563, a group of English laws called the 'Statute of Artificers' was passed by the government of Elizabeth I, regulating the supply of labour, setting wages for certain classes of worker, and disallowing apprentices to look for work outside their parish, effectively restricting the free movement of workers. For the masons, this was particularly difficult, as they were restricted in travelling to other areas to repair and maintain Churches and other buildings. Other trades could still survive by serving their community; the Glovers, Brewers and the Smiths for example could ply their trade from a fixed location within the town or city, but those crafts relating to the specialist building trades who depended on travelling to other areas, were restricted. In effect, the powers held by the craft guilds were transferred to the English state.

The effects of the Reformation led nineteenth century Masonic historians, such as W. H. Rylands to comment that:

'The Reformation had a disastrous effect on the system upon which the guilds of Masons were based. The whole was changed. It is not surprising, therefore, to find that many of the operative lodges died out, and the members for the most part were probably scattered over the whole country. Some, however, as independent bodies, survived the storm, and lasted for a considerable period. Of course, their use for ruling the trade generally of a district or town had largely, if not entirely, passed away. The speculative element lasted, and, in some instances at least, if they did not take entire possession of the lodge, they appear to have assisted in keeping it alive.'[125]

The entries of masons as freemen in Chester for example seem to support this, with no masons appearing as freemen from the 1520s until the late 1650s. With the admission being based on whether their father was a freeman or apprenticeship, and with the cost of the privileges attached to the enfranchisement, the masons' absence from the Freemen Rolls during this 130 year period certainly reflects a downturn in demand for the trade in Chester, a downturn which would have affected the number of masons working in the area.

Masonic historian Neville Barker Cryer in his work on York lodges during this period has also stated that there was an 'almost complete demise of the local building site lodges between 1530 and 1630'.[126] Though in York during this period, despite a handful of masons who became freemen – including a small number who were listed as 'freemaysons' – the trade decayed. Barker Cryer stated in York Mysteries Revealed; 'the list of working masons began to diminish after 1540', on the whole due to the fact that the religious centres such as the Abbeys and the chantry chapels closed.[127] The subsequent Reformation and Civil War took its toll on the Minster, and it was not until the nineteenth and twentieth centuries that extensive repair work was carried out.

There are countless stonemasons' marks to see in the Minster. Pentacles can be seen on various stones throughout the interior, and indeed, the building has an excellent variation of different stonemasons' marks that have been studied by Masonic and medieval historians. There are magnificent stained glass windows dating from the eighteenth century that display Masonic symbolism, such as the window showing the creation, with God being displayed in the centre as the Grand Architect, holding a compass.

The Minster has attracted many Freemasons over the centuries, one such renowned local Mason being John Browne, who became a member of the York 'Union' Lodge in 1825, becoming Worshipful Master in 1831 and again in 1837.[128] Browne was an artist who was deeply interested in the Minster, drawing its ornaments, plans and drawing studies of the medieval

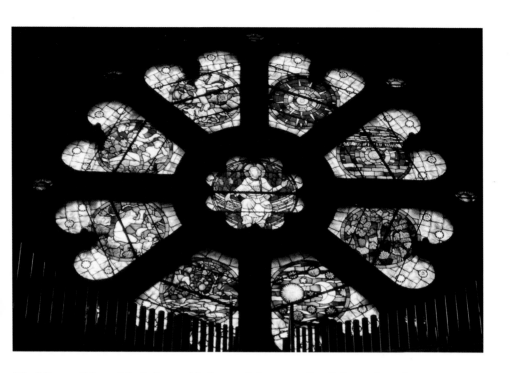

*The Minster 'Masonic' windows with the one below revealing Solomon's seal.*

painted glass. These appeared in his acclaimed *History of the Minster*, part 1 appearing in 1838, a work that was finally completed with part 33 in 1847; the full *History* encompassing two large volumes.[129] Browne was also intensely interested in archaeology, presenting a paper to the Yorkshire Philosophical Society in 1826,[130] and he conducted a study on a hoard of early medieval coins found in York, which was later purchased by the Society.[131] Browne was also famous for drawing many sketches of the local area, continuing the link between local York artists and writers with Freemasonry. Indeed, Browne was not unlike Francis Drake in his fascination of the history of York, with fellow member of the Yorkshire Philosophical Society George Benson stating that 'without Browne's work on the Minster we should know little of its real meaning and significance'.[132]

Another Freemason strongly associated with the Minster was John Camidge. Camidge

was baptised in December 1734 and was the founder of a dynasty of York musicians, John being the Minster organist from 1756-1799. John was a member of the Apollo Lodge and the Good Humour Club (the Doctor's Club), and he composed a hymn for the lodge which was sung in the chapel in 1781, the year when he became Worshipful Master. John also founded the York Musical Society and he could play the violin; playing the Theatre Royal during the early 1770s. His son Matthew continued in his father's illustrious footsteps and became Minster organist in 1799 until his retirement in 1842. Matthew's son John then took over and was the Minster organist from 1842-1848.[133]

*John Browne, early 19th century historian of the Minster and member of the York 'Union' Lodge. The photograph was taken by his son, Henry Browne.* (Courtesy of the library, Duncombe Place)

*The Minster stonemason's marks.*

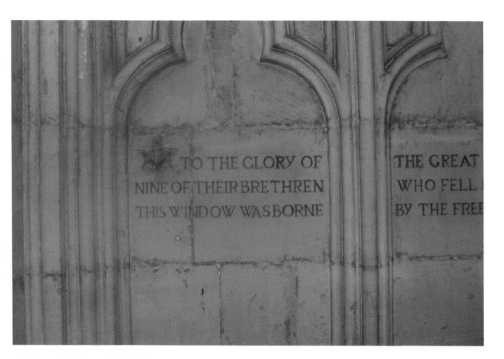

*A Masonic Memorial in the Minster.*

## Bedern Hall

In December 2005, around 200 years after the York Grand Lodge had disappeared; a group of Freemasons came together and called themselves the Grand Lodge of All England held at York. A convocation of the Grand Lodge took place at Bedern Hall at York on 12 June 2006, preceded by a meeting of St John's Lodge; the Grand Lodge installing, investing and proclaiming its Grand Master Elect John Gordon Graves, who then invested his Grand Officers.[134] The Grand Lodge had, for a brief number of years, a rather active online presence, with an impressive website and lively discussions on certain forums. Their Grand Secretary - actor Peter J. Clatworthy - put forward how the revived Grand Lodge was based, like the old York Grand Lodge, on the Edwin legend and, in essence, that they were a legitimate revival.[135]

However, they soon attracted criticism

and despite a new lodge called St John's Lodge being founded in Dayton, Ohio in the US on 21 November 2007[136] and a reported meeting held in the Crypt of York Minster in June 2008, where the Grand Master received 'The Order of Service to Freemasonry' from the Chancellor of The Grand Loge De France, Jean-Claude Hertz,[137] they had completely disappeared from the internet by 2010. However, they are still very much in operation at the time of writing; becoming even more secretive, they still claim to be a constitutional restoration of the Grand Lodge of All England. They meet in both York and Winchester, practice seven degrees and accept women as members.[138] This revived York Grand Lodge, thus uses an updated constitution and has the principles of the old York Grand Lodge, being in a way, similar to the revival witnessed in 1761; though back then of course, actual surviving members of the original Grand Lodge were directly involved. Indeed, only four members of this new organisation were ever publically mentioned online,[139] though there seem to be many more that are active privately.[140]

Bedern Hall, known locally as the Bedern

– an Anglo-Saxon word meaning 'house of prayer', was a very apt meeting place for the twenty first century revival of the York Grand Lodge; a medieval building dating back to the fourteenth century, the hall once being part of the College of the Vicars Choral. The building was tied to the Minster and used as a dining hall for the College from around the 1390s until the mid-1600s. The Vicars Choral sang services in the Minster, but with the Reformation and then the Civil War, the Bedern became the location of a school and then tenements, becoming overcrowded with Irish immigrants escaping the famine and in need of repair by the mid-1800s. More recently, the site of the hall was used as a bakery and a pork butchers, before being restored and renovated in the 1980s. It is now the present home of some of the surviving Guilds: the Company of Cordwainers, the Gild of Freemen and the York Guild of Building, and the hall can be hired for weddings and events. It was at one such event that the modern revived York Grand Lodge met in 2006, re-launching them as an alternative to the UGLE.[141]

*The Bedern, scene of the meeting of the revived Grand Lodge of All England in York in June 2006.*

# WIDER CONSIDERATIONS: COUNTRY ESTATES AND HALLS ASSOCIATED WITH YORK FREEMASONS

**The Commemorative Arch, Parlington Hall, Aberford near Leeds**

There are some country estates in Yorkshire connected to local Freemasonry and are worth mentioning here, in particular Parlington Hall, which belonged to Sir Thomas Gascoigne, 8th Baronet who was Grand Master of the York Grand Lodge from 1771-2. Sir Thomas Gascoigne was born in Cambrai, France, on 7 March 1745, and died in 1810. Typical of the rebellious Jacobite York Grand Masters; he was an avid supporter of the American War of Independence, and built a commemorative arch to the American victory on his estate at Parlington, the arch being influenced by the Arch to Constantine in Rome. Gascoigne was also a Catholic, but he was received into the Church of England and became a Member of Parliament for Thirsk, Malton and Arundel in the 1780s and 1790s. Despite this, he built St. Wilfred's Church near to his estate in Aberford, for the Catholics of the area.[142]

Gascoigne later married Mary, daughter of James Shuttleworth of Gawthorpe and the widow of Sir Charles Turner. His only son from this marriage, also called Thomas, died tragically while out hunting, just months before his own death. Though the main part of Parlington Hall has been demolished, the arch can still be seen on the grounds of the old estate, and is another reminder of how some Freemasons celebrated classical architecture. There is a local legend that the Prince Regent, later George IV, visited Parlington and was due to meet Sir Thomas Gascoigne for luncheon, but on encountering the arch, and once informed of the purpose behind the building of the monument, the Prince Regent, who incidentally was also a Freemason – though of the 'Modern' persuasion – refused to continue. The inscription on the arch reads 'Liberty in N. America Triumphant MDCCLXXXIII'.[143]

**Naburn Hall, Naburn, near York**

Naburn Hall was the residence of the Palmes family, John and Georges Palmes both serving as Grand Masters of the York Grand Lodge. Both were descended from a staunch Yorkshire Catholic family, one of ancient lineage with links to the Tudor dynasty and the aforementioned Fairfax family. Both John and George Palmes joined the York Grand Lodge soon after its 1761 revival, their Catholicism and lineage would have certainly been well known in the locality of York; John and George being fitting Grand Masters for the newly resurrected York Grand Lodge.[144] John Palmes Esq. served as Grand Master from 1765-1766, and George Palmes Esq., the elder brother, served as Grand Master in 1768. George was the head of the Naburn estate until his death in 1774 when it passed to his younger brother John, who died in 1783.[145]The hall, which was rebuilt in 1735 and altered and enlarged during the nineteenth century, still survives and remained in the Palmes family until the death of Commander George Bryan Palmes in 1974.

**Bramham Park**

Bramham Park was built for the Rt. Hon. Robert Benson 1st Lord Bingley, who was born c.1676 in Wakefield. Benson became MP for Thetford in Norfolk from 1702-1705, before becoming MP for York from 1705-1713. He was President of the Old York Lodge in 1707, and became Commissioner for the Treasury in 1710, Chancellor of the Exchequer in 1711 and Ambassador to Spain in 1713. He was also a director of the South Seas Company from 1711-1715, his political persuasion being that of a moderate Tory. Benson had been influenced by classical architecture on the Grand Tour, particularly that of Palladio, and built the Baroque style Bramham Park in 1698. He died in April 1731 and was buried in Westminster Abbey.[146]

## Newby Park

Newby Park is a Palladian manor house built in 1718 by Colen Campbell for Sir William Robinson 1st Baronet. Robinson was born on 19 November 1655, and like his fellow illustrious Presidents of the Old York Lodge, acquired numerous offices; he was MP for Northallerton from 1689-1695, served as High Sheriff in 1689, and was MP for York from 1698-1722. He became Baronet of Newby on 13 February 1690, and Lord Mayor of York in 1700. He was President of the Old York Lodge from 1708 until 1710, and was considered a Whig by Lord Carmarthen. Robinson died on 22 December 1736.[147] Newby Park was inspired by Palladio's Villa Emo at Fanzolo; with the temple-like portico and a perfect square plan to the building – revealing architectural precision that can also be seen with Burlington's Chiswick House. The hall is now the site of Queen Mary's School set within Baldersby Park near Thirsk.

## Hawkesworth Hall

Sir Walter Hawkesworth, 2nd Baronet, was born in 1683 and was first seen as serving as President of the Old York Lodge in 1711. He was High Sheriff for Yorkshire in 1721, and he made many alterations to Hawkesworth Hall and its gardens, situated in the village of Hawksworth. He served as President again from 1720-1724/5, and died in York in March 1735.

## Skellow Grange, near Doncaster, former home of Freemason and writer Godfrey Higgins

Godfrey Higgins was born in 1772 and died in 1833. He resided at Skellow Grange near Doncaster, the house having been built by his father, living the life of a comfortable country squire. Higgins was educated at Cambridge and studied law, becoming a Yorkshire magistrate and a reformer, playing a leading role in uncovering the abuse of the patients at the York Lunatic Asylum. He supported the building of the Yorkshire Museum, was interested in archaeology, and as a member of the Society of Antiquaries, Higgins explored the hidden mysteries of the past, publishing his celebrated work *The Celtic Druids* in three parts between 1827-1829. As a Freemason who held an intense interest in ancient religions and mythology, he was attracted to the York Grand Lodge, Higgins believing that the Grand Lodge at York had an older lineage, its rites and ritual belonging to a more ancient and antiquated culture. His celebrated work *Anacalypsis* still manages to be controversial today, dividing historians in the way the work has influenced modern day theosophy and occultism. Skellow Grange still exists and is now a residential care home called Skellow Hall.

## Nunnington Hall and Church

Nunnington Hall is worth a mention here, even though a known Mason did not own it the Hall was the residence of Viscount Preston who was a leading Jacobite. Preston was fiercely loyal to James II after the Glorious Revolution of 1688, and secretly plotted for James in the early 1690s. Preston was arrested, tried for high treason and sentenced to death, but the sentence was not carried out and Preston was allowed to return to Nunnington. Preston's monument, which mentions his Jacobite stance, can be seen in Nunnington Church, Preston being a prominent example of the strong Jacobite sympathies that existed amongst some of the leading Yorkshire families, families such as the Palmes and Gascoignes.

# LODGES UNDER YORK AND OTHER OLD YORKSHIRE LODGES OF INTEREST

Yorkshire has some of the oldest lodges in the country, and as a result, some of these lodges practice rituals, which, so it is claimed, date back to before the union of the Antients and Moderns in 1813. The York Lodge No.236 practices one of these rituals – the York Working – and it is said that the ritual 'is most likely to be that of the Moderns with perhaps a little influence from the Antients and possibly some from the Grand Lodge of All England.'[148] Other lodges throughout Yorkshire work variations of the York Working such as De Grey and Ripon Lodge No.837. Another old Yorkshire ritual is the 'Humber Use' used in Humber Lodge No.57, which meets in Hull. The ritual is based upon the writings of a certain Bro. Bartholomew Samuel Oates, who was initiated into the lodge in 1856, though the later nineteenth century scholar F. W. De Velling commented that the language used in the ritual 'is the standard English of the 18th Century'.[149] The Humber Lodge was an Antient lodge that had acquired a Warrant from a Liverpool lodge in 1809, though the original date of the Warrant is 1756. The name of the Hull lodge was 'Ancient Knight Templars', but in 1810, it was changed to Humber Lodge. The lodge currently meets at the Masonic Hall in Kingston-Upon-Hull.[150]

Lodge of Probity No.61 in Halifax is a very old lodge, being founded in 1738, its early history being somewhat entwined with the York Grand Lodge; a lodge at the Talbot Inn, Halifax under the York Grand Lodge was founded on 22 May 1738. This lodge however, did not last long at all; it first met on 4 July, but on 1 August, just less than a month later; the 'Modern' Lodge of Probity No.61 was constituted, meeting at the Bull's Head in Halifax. Interestingly, one of the members of the 'York' lodge; James Hamilton, was described as the landlord of the Bull's Head, so one could assume that the Lodge of Probity, the oldest surviving lodge in Yorkshire today, replaced the local 'York' lodge outright, and one member at least continued his Freemasonry with the Moderns.[151]

There are no complete membership lists available for the Lodge of Probity before 1762. But its first lodge history, written in 1888, discusses the conflict between the York Grand Lodge and the Modern Grand Lodge during this time, quoting William Preston, who commented that, the venturing into the West Riding of Yorkshire by the Grand Lodge in London:

'was considered a third encroachment on the jurisdiction of the Grand Lodge in York, and so widened the original breach between the brethren in the north and the south of England, that from henceforward all further correspondence between the two Grand Lodges totally ceased.'

Despite this tension, there is evidence that the Lodge of Probity 're-initiated' members from the Antient and possibly the York Grand Lodge as the eighteenth century progressed.[152] The Lodge of Probity now meets at the Southwood Club in Halifax.

The York Grand Lodge, as we have seen, was revived in 1761 when the founding of a Modern lodge by a company of actors in the Punch Bowl Tavern caused something of a stir.[153] At the official re-launching of the York Grand Lodge, a number of brethren were present from the Modern lodge, some of whom became active members of the revived York Grand Lodge, such as John Tasker and Malby Beckwith.[154] The lodge at the Punch Bowl effectively switched allegiance to 'York', though the minutes of this Punch Bowl Lodge end abruptly in January 1763, the lodge seemingly having come to a natural end. With the actors being absent for a number of months in the year due to their theatre work, the more prominent members such as John Palmes, Malby Beckwith and John Tasker became directly involved in the Grand Lodge. The other lodge founded in the Punch Bowl was the French Prisoners of war lodge in 1762, which only lasted a year.

The revived Grand Lodge soon re-established itself and seemed to continue where it left off. It began attracting prominent men from the city and started to take part in civic activities, such as in 1767 when it was proposed that the Grand Master and members of the Grand Lodge should attend the laying of the first stone of a new bridge being built across the River Foss. The architect was none other than the Senior Grand

*The York Grand Lodge resurrected in 1761.*

Warden – Brother Joseph Atkinson.[155]

The following year, two prominent local gentlemen became members; Sir Walter Vavasour and Sir Thomas Gascoigne, and when Gascoigne was installed as Grand Master on 27 December 1770, during the celebration of St John, a procession of the Grand Lodge took place which included 120 Brethren accompanied by a band of music. To the sound of the ringing bells of St Martin's in Coney Street, the procession left the York Tavern at 9 o'clock in the morning, and arrived at St John's at Micklegate for a sermon, before returning back to dine at the York Tavern, after which, at 5 o'clock, the Grand Master was duly installed with the other Grand Officers. The style of regalia was defined; Grand Lodge Officers wore aprons of Mazarine blue, lined and bound, Stewards wore aprons of red silk, lined and bound, Master Masons wore aprons of white silk, lined and bound, and Fellow Crafts also wore white aprons, but not lined and bound.[156] This was a show of strength by a confident independent Grand Lodge; a Grand Lodge that was growing, and with that growth, came an interest in establishing more new lodges in their territory.

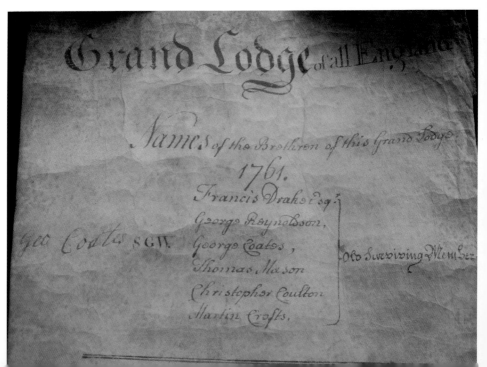

The majority of the new lodges that were founded by the revived Grand Lodge were located in Yorkshire, but an ambitious effort at expansion was conducted during the Grand Lodge's later phase, and as we shall see, lodges were founded in Cheshire and Lancashire. Indeed, it is at local level where we can best examine how the York Grand Lodge actually worked; its lodges working the York ritual termed the 'York Working'. Some York lodges vanished without trace after a brief life, while others were replaced by either Modern or Antient lodges; these new lodges having a number of brethren from the pre-existing York lodge, meeting in the same place, using the same furniture and, in some cases, claiming to practice a variation of the York Working.

A York lodge in Scarborough had been recorded as early as 1705, and though this had been a special lodge to admit six men, a second lodge under York was mentioned meeting there on 16 August 1762, at the Turk's Head. This revival of a Scarborough lodge did not last long despite having established traditions in the coastal town, and seems to have ended around 1768. A letter sent to the Junior Grand Warden at York by Thomas Hart in 1772, described what had happened to the lodge, bemoaning how the owner of the Turk's Head – a certain William Jefferson - had the lodge jewels in his keeping, and would not surrender them until the York Grand Lodge had been consulted.

According to Hart's letter, the lodge at Scarborough had been thriving but had sadly begun to wane. Jefferson had admitted two or three of his friends:

'who seem'd to prefer a large copious bowl of Punch to the inestimable mystery wch in time tired the most serious part of ye community so much that rather than have their purses deeply dipt into; that ye Lodge was forsook since which Jefferson has left the House & remov'd to a private one...'

It appeared that drinking had become the central part of the lodge evening, and the lodge closed as a result. The jewels and punch bowl finally found their way to a certain Mr Hall, whose widow passed them on to a Bro. Steel of the Scarborough lodge, who finally passed them back to the York Grand Lodge. The punch bowl however, is now missing.[157]

A lodge at the Royal Oak at Ripon under the York Grand Lodge was meeting by August 1769, and its Brethren took part in the Grand Lodge procession at York in December 1770, when Sir Thomas Gascoigne was installed as Grand Master. By 1776 however, William Askwith, the landlord of the Royal Oak and Worshipful Master of the Ripon Lodge visited the Apollo Lodge in York - a Modern lodge - where he 'desired to be made a mason under the constitution of England in this lodge'. Thus on 22 June in the same year, the Ripon lodge was replaced by a Modern lodge, which met at the same inn. This new Modern lodge had four members that had belonged to the previous York lodge. Royal Oak Lodge No.495 lasted until 1828 when it was erased, but De Grey and Ripon Lodge No.837, which was constituted in October 1860, still survives and still claims to work some of the old York Working.[158]

On 21 November 1769, a lodge at the Crown Inn at Knaresborough was constituted under the York Grand Lodge and like the Ripon lodge, Brethren from the Knaresborough lodge attended the York Grand Lodge procession in December 1770 for the installation of Sir Thomas Gascoigne. Again, the landlord of the Inn where the lodge was to meet was involved. Robert Revell had been balloted and admitted in the May, and he was raised in the October with two other men; the Rev. Charles Kedar and William Bateson, all three being on the petition for the new Knaresborough lodge on the very same evening they became Master Masons. By January 1785 however, the Modern Newtonian Lodge No.499 had been constituted, meeting at the Elephant and Castle. Four of the petitioners for this new lodge had been members of the local York lodge, and it seems that, like the Halifax and Ripon lodges, a number of the brethren had opted for the Moderns.[159] The Newtonian Lodge was erased in December 1851.[160]

A petition to the York Grand Lodge for

a lodge to be held at the sign of the Duke of Devonshire Flying Childers in Goose Lane, Macclesfield in Cheshire, was presented on 24 September 1770.[161] However, this Cheshire lodge did not last long, as an Antient lodge was meeting at the same inn four years later, wholly displacing the 'York' lodge.[162] It seemed like a very ambitious attempt at establishing a lodge so far away from its administrative centre in York, but, as a Warrant was requested to set a lodge up there by a Brother Abraham Sampson, the York Grand Lodge responded positively and pro-actively; Sampson and the 'York' Brethren involved in setting up the new lodge had been barred from visiting an existing Antient lodge in Macclesfield. It seemed during this period, with three Grand Lodges to choose from, disgruntled brethren could petition the rival bodies in the hope of starting a new rival lodge. The Macclesfield 'York' lodge disappeared and the Antient Lodge No.189 began meeting in the same inn, being constituted on 7 June 1774, removing to the Golden Lion twenty years later.[163] Sampson was next heard from trying to start a 'York' lodge in London, promising to send the 3 guineas still owed for the granting of the constitution for the Macclesfield lodge, and the a further 3 guineas for the London lodge. No money appears to have been sent, and nothing further was done.

In March 1773, a petition to the York Grand Lodge was made to form a lodge at Hovingham, and Rev. Ralph Tunstall from the village became central to this lodge and was to be involved in a later lodge at Snainton after he had moved to nearby Malton. The Hovingham lodge seems to have disintegrated, and by 1776, it was no more. However, a lodge, held at the New Inn at Snainton, was constituted at the end of 1778, though there is scant information concerning how long it actually existed. A tollgate had been erected at the small village of Snainton and the New Inn was opened in 1776 as a staging post to accommodate weary travellers on the main road from Malton to Scarborough. The man behind the petition was none other than the aforementioned Rev. Ralph Tunstall, who had been a member of the defunct Hovingham lodge, though this lodge seemed to follow the same fate.

The petition to form the Druidical Lodge at Rotherham was presented to the York Grand Lodge in October 1778, and it became quite a successful lodge, lasting at least into the mid-1790s, if not beyond. Its first meeting on 22 December 1778, was followed by a procession to Rotherham parish church by the Masons of the lodge and members of the York Grand Lodge. This was an official celebration of the new lodge and a very public statement, as the Grand Master himself was present. William Blanchard subsequently published a sermon, delivered by the Grand Chaplain, the Rev. John Parker.[164]

John Hassall, a wine and spirit merchant, was a founding member of Druidical Lodge, and his later adventures became important to spreading the influence of the York Grand Lodge further afield. Hassall was probably born in Chester and had originally been an Irish Mason, being a member of Lodge No.375, which was based in Dublin. His fortunes took a downturn when he was imprisoned for debt at York Castle in 1780, Hassall writing a somewhat moving letter to the York Grand Lodge asking for help.[165] It appears that the Grand Lodge assisted Hassall, and after his release he moved to Manchester for ventures new. Another founding member of Druidical was Attorney Josiah Beckwith, who had the task of visiting the Earl of Effingham on behalf of the Grand Lodge, approaching him with the offer of becoming Grand Master in October 1779, an offer the Earl turned down.[166]

The Druidical Lodge kept excellent records during their first few years and during a meeting of the lodge on 26 March 1779, an example of the antagonism between the York and Modern Grand Lodges was displayed when it discussed the situation of Mr James Hamer who had been proposed as a member, but had since been admitted into the Rose and Crown Lodge No.277 - a Modern lodge in Sheffield. It was

*A page discussing a meeting of the Grand Lodge in February 1780.*

...ation being made to the Most Worshipful Grand —
...ter of all England for Leave that the Free Macoons —
...t in Procession attend the funeral of Mr. Martin —
...t the Elder deceased, late an Honorary Member of the —
...Lodge of all England, He was pleased to comply
...request And thereupon by his Order the Tyler
...to invite the Brethren severally, with a Notice
...whereof here follows,

All Free and Accepted Macoons in York, By Order
of Francis Smyth Esqr. Grand Master, are —
desired to attend in Procession on Friday this fourth
of february 1780 at the funeral of Our late Worthy
and respected Brother Martin Croft the Elder
some time past an Honorary Member of the —
Grand Lodge of all England.
The Brethren are to assemble at the York Tavern
at half past Two O Clock in the Afternoon, Dressed
in Mourning with White Stockings Gloves & Aprons.
                                        John Browne, G. S.

...day the fourth Day of february 1780 the Brethren
...led in the Grand Lodge Room at half past two o
...the Afternoon pursuant to Notice, And a Lodge
...ned in the third Degree at which the Most
...ful Grand Master presided in Person And there
...sent the Officers and Brethren mentioned in the
...itten Order of Procession. All the Brethren being
...bled about four o Clock (The Officers having their
...and they and all the Brethren being in Mourning
...rons and White Gloves, And having each a Sprig
...reen in his Hand) soon afterwards proceeded —
...Stonegate to the Parish Church of the Holy Trinity
...Court, Receiving into the Procession the Deceased
...Corps and Mourners attendant at the Door of —
...in Petergate.

The form of Procession was as follows
...cers and Members of the Grand Lodge taking the right Hand.

Rich. Jackson { Sword Bearers } Rich. Baynes.

Willr. Smith { Stewards with } Wm. Stabley.
             { Mourning Rods }
The Brethren two and two went Arm in Arm.

Joseph Atkinson ——————— John Croft ——
                              & Dr Mitchell.

ordered that he should be 'for ever expelled' from Druidical 'and excluded from this Society either as a Member or a Visiting Brother'. However, when Hamer was passed in the Rose and Crown Lodge on 14 May 1779, Bro Joseph Antt of the York Grand Lodge actually visited the Modern lodge.[167] Away from the watchful eyes of the York hierarchy, friendly interaction between Masons of the two Grand Lodges could take place.[168]

The Druidical Lodge met at the Red Lion Inn, and though York lodges appeared to have not been officially numbered, this lodge was later given the number of 109, perhaps as a further means of recognition in a country where all Modern and Antient lodges had numbers to distinguish them. Later in its life, the lodge developed a relationship with the Modern North Nottinghamshire Lodge No.587, which later reformed into Phoenix Lodge.[169] The Tyler from Druidical brought the jewels for the use of the constitution of the new lodge. However, the new Modern lodge appears to have kept the jewels, and in June 1792, 'It was ordered, that the Secretary write a letter to the Druidical Lodge at Rotherham...to thank the Brothers for the loan of their jewels'.[170]

Three years after this, Rev. Beaumont Broadbent who had originally joined Druidical, asked to be re-made and raised in the Modern lodge. Interestingly, the good Reverend was described in the minutes of North Nottinghamshire Lodge as 'being of the Antient Freemasonry'. It was noted that he had 'requested to be made a Mason and raised to the third Degree according to our form...'[171] A discount was also given to the Reverend in respect of his already being a Mason, as it was decided that he should 'be exempt from the fees for raising to the Second & Third Degrees.'[172] The Brethren of North Nottinghamshire Lodge reformed as Phoenix Lodge in Rotherham in July 1808, though four of its listed nine members had previously been in Druidical.[173] Additionally, Phoenix Lodge now possessed the original 'York' Warrant and possibly some of their furniture, suggesting that the various surviving members of Druidical had merged with the Modern lodge

sometime earlier.[174] This lodge was only erased in 1838.

Arthur Edward Waite, in his *Secret Tradition in Freemasonry* discussed how Godfrey Higgins, sometime before 1836, went to York and 'applied to the only survivor of the Lodge who shewed me, from the documents which he possessed, that the Druidical Lodge, or Chapter of Royal Arch Masons, or Templar Encampment was held for the last time in the Crypt [of the Cathedral at York] on Sunday, May 27th, 1778.' Waite quoted this last survivor of the York Grand Lodge as being Grand Secretary William Blanchard, and the gathering in the crypt by the Royal Arch Brethren did take place. A Chapter at Rotherham was actually petitioned for in 1780, so the Druidical brethren could work the Royal Arch degree in their hometown,[175] and a Royal Encampment of Knights Templar was also held in Rotherham so the Brethren could practice the fifth degree. Druidical may have survived to 1795, the year Broadbent was re-made in the Modern North Nottinghamshire lodge, but by 1808, the remnants of Druidical were to be found in the Modern Phoenix Lodge, a fate which reflected some of the earlier 'York' lodges.

Despite the apparent success reflected in its expansion, the York Grand Lodge did experience some setbacks; in 1774, attendance at Grand Lodge meetings had dropped, but it steadily rose again to around 25-30 by 1778, probably due to the introduction of harsher punishments for non-attendance. This can be seen in a Grand Lodge meeting in May 1776, when the Grand Lodge ordered that Brother T. Bewlay had to pay all the arrears due from him if he did not attend the next Lodge night, his membership would be discontinued and he would be banned from visiting! The threat worked, and Brother Bewlay duly turned up at the next meeting, going on to serve as Junior Grand Warden.

The confidence of the Grand Lodge was certainly shaken when a Modern lodge once again was founded in York itself, and to make matters worse, disgruntled York Grand Lodge members founded the lodge. Apollo Lodge was founded in 1773, and became somewhat of a haven for various ex-members and prospective initiates

*A page of the minute book revealing a funeral procession that included the York 'Union' Lodge, the Apollo Lodge and the York Grand Lodge.*

Chris. Lockwood ——————— Bagley

Alexanr. Smith
Secretary of the Union Lodge

John Stephenson { Wardens of the Union Lodge } Jos. Jones

John Preston
Master of the Union Lodge

Alex.r Cumming ———————— James Lamb.
Wm Clayton ———————— Thos. Thackeray
Fran.s Hunt ———————— Wm. Nicholson
Thos. Allanson ———————— Robt. Flaxby
Wm Staveley ———————— John Sanderson
James Oram ———————— Willm Crofs.
John Hicks ——— Members ——— Wm Blanchard.
John Hampston ——— of ——— Mark Anthy Robinson.
John Firth ——— the ——— Ralph Dodsworth.
Thos Willans ——— Grand ——— John Consitt.
John Coupland ——— Lodge. ——— Rich.d Willbor

George Coates.

John Browne ——— Secretarys with Rolls ——— Jos.a Oldfield.
George Kitson ——— Treasurers ——— Thos. Swann
Fran.s Clubley ——— Junior Wardens ——— James Rule.
Thos. Beckwith ——— Senior Wardens ——— John Camidge
Willm. Siddall ——— Past Masters ——— Thos. Atkinson
Robt. Lakeland ——— Deputys ——— Willm. Spencer.

Deacon with a mourning staff
{ The Ancient Constitution Rolls and
Ensigns of Masonry on a Cushion
carried by Brother John Dalton and
covered with Black Cloth. }
Deacon with a mourning staff

Smyth
Grand Master

Revd. John Parker Grand Chaplain —

This Pall was supported
Ward in their Gauntles And
with two Swords crossed
{ The Body }
by the Commoners of Monk
a Square and Compasses
was placed thereon.

——— Mourners
among whom were Bror. Rich.d Garland & Markintosh

Richard Dawson

Leonard Watson { Stewards with mourning Rods } Nath.l Frobisher
John Jennings { Tylers with mourning Rods } Robt. Mountain

55

who had been rejected by 'York'. For example, surgeon and ex-'Yorkite' William Spencer was a founding member and the first Worshipful Master of Apollo; another recognisable 'York' name was jeweller Malby Beckwith, who served as the new lodge Secretary, and merchants Richard Garland and Joseph Braint were also ex-'Yorkites'. Thomas Clifton was a 'York' reject who found a home at Apollo, being proposed as a member in November 1783.[176] There may have been a number of reasons why Spencer, Beckwith, Garland and the other members of Apollo who once belonged to 'York' had left; Spencer and Beckwith had previously been members of Punch Bowl Lodge, but despite Spencer having risen to the dizzy heights of Deputy Grand Master of 'York', a Modern lodge offered a wider networking system, and as there were restrictions on 'York' Brethren visiting 'Modern' lodges, leaving 'York' became the only option for some.[177]

Spencer became Deputy Provincial Grand Master of Yorkshire soon after Apollo was founded, and the lodge certainly sought prestige; with Provincial Grand Lodge Officers being routinely elected from Apollo. It also attracted high status visitors such as Provincial Grand Master Sir Thomas Tancred and the Grand Secretary James Heseltine. Ex-'Yorkite' Richard Garland followed Spencer as Deputy Provincial Grand Master in 1780, but he began to drift into debt, resigned his Provincial Office in 1786, and stopped attending Apollo the following year.[178] In 1788, he was accused by Alfred Lodge in Wetherby of not having passed money onto Grand Lodge that they had given to him. Scandal was averted when Apollo members reimbursed the money to Alfred Lodge, but this seemed to mark a turning point for Apollo; money matters had been discussed previously by the lodge and Apollo entered a period of decline. Garland himself became bankrupt in 1795.[179] As Apollo slowly declined, so did the Yorkshire Province, with Provincial Grand Secretary and Apollo member John Watson virtually working alone to keep the management of the Yorkshire Province running up until the opening years of the nineteenth century. Watson had written to the London based Grand Lodge in the February of 1802, stating that:

'The Lodge [Apollo] has not met for some years past. Our P.G.Master is so very infirm, as renders him unable to attend to the Duties of his Office, and the Lodge deserted. I was induced, in the hope of its revival, to take the whole weight upon my shoulders and have for some time back found it too heavy for me, as such, I was under the necessity of resigning.'[180]

Watson however stayed in the Office for a few more years and was a regular visitor to the 'Modern' York 'Union' Lodge, with Watson sometimes being listed as 'of the Apollo Lodge'. It was only in 1803 that the Lodge of Probity in Halifax corresponded with the York 'Union' Lodge in regards to 're-establishing' the Provincial Grand Lodge in Yorkshire.[181] By this time, as we shall see, the York Grand Lodge was in terminal decline itself, and the Apollo Lodge seems to have ceased working sometime around 1817, the same year that the large Yorkshire Province was divided in two.[182]

The York Grand Lodge did however go from strength to strength during the ensuing decades after its revival; it was founding new lodges, it still attracted leading local gentlemen such as Robert Sinclair and Edward Wolley, and they had even courted the Earl of Effingham as a potential Grand Master in 1779.[183] The York Grand Lodge was also practising five degrees by the late 1770s, and their unique form of ritual coupled with their boasted ancient traditions certainly played a part in attracting the attention of various Masons to their style of working. One Mason in particular - William Preston - would cement the success of the York Grand Lodge during this period, by rebelling against the Modern Grand Lodge and being a leading figure in a new rebel Grand Lodge which was proudly attached to York: the Grand Lodge of All England South of the River Trent. There were three lodges under this new Grand Lodge; Lodge of Antiquity, Lodge of Perseverance and Triumph, which was constituted at the Queen's Head Tavern in Holborn on 9 August 1779, and Lodge of Perfect Observance, which was constituted at the Mitre Tavern in Fleet Street on 15 November 1779. The Lodge of Perfect Observance in particular was a very interesting lodge; made up of mainly European Masons, it practiced the Rite of Seven Degrees under Peter Lambert De Lintot, who became Worshipful Master of the lodge, De Lintot going on to petition the Grand Lodge of Scotland to gain recognition for the Rite.[184] Despite a promising start, Preston's rebel Grand Lodge only lasted ten years, the remaining brethren apologising and re-joining the Modern's in 1789. The York Grand Lodge however was still expanding, gaining an influence over the border into Lancashire, where John Hassall founded a Royal Encampment of Knight Templar in Manchester in 1786 and went on to found Lodge of Fortitude in Hollinwood near Oldham in 1790. Hassall seems to have recruited Masons from a Modern lodge called the Lodge of Friendship in Oldham, Masons who were perhaps attracted to a 'York' lodge which offered a five degree system; the three Craft degrees followed by the Royal Arch and Knight Templar degrees, a pathway practiced in a different 'York' style.

However, another lodge was in the process of being constituted after the Lodge of Fortitude — its constitution being mentioned in the last minute entry we have of the York Grand Lodge on 23 August 1792, though which lodge in particular remains a mystery. Barker Cryer mentions that there was an opinion that this lodge could have been the Lodge of Hope in Bradford.[185] This still exists and has in its possession a version of the Old Charges, referred to as the old York Manuscript Constitution or the Hope MS, which has been dated to c.1680; Masonic historian William Hughan likening it to the York MS of 1693.[186]

The Lodge of Hope however, was constituted under the Moderns on 23 March 1794, although it had originally conferred its Mark degree under the old York Manuscript Constitution.[187] In the Mark Register, which began in 1852, there is a list of certain Brethren that had been carried forward from a now lost older register, and amongst these names was Brother R.M. Scholefield, who was a Mark Mason from the Lodge of Hope during the opening decades of the nineteenth century. Scholefield was deputed by the lodge to attend the foundation of the UGLE in 1813, in order to ascertain the position of the Hope Mark degree under the new regulations. He then returned to Bradford with an arrangement that the Lodge of Hope could continue to practice the Mark degree as conferred by the old York Manuscript Constitution, which it still practiced independently until 1873 when it finally joined the Mark Grand Lodge, and still meets as the Old York TI Lodge.[188]

This instance of the Lodge of Hope Mark degree being conferred by a York Manuscript Constitution could be an example of a lodge, which in seeking higher degrees, was, like the brethren of the Lodge of Friendship in Oldham and the Royal Encampment in Manchester, able to cross the Grand Lodge divide without prejudice. There seems to be a consensus within the history of Lodge of Hope that the lodge may be related to an older working lodge in the area, and despite being constituted as a 'Modern' lodge, it is clear that there was an influence from the York Grand Lodge. At the first meeting of the Lodge of Hope, a number of Brethren visited from Lodge of Harmony, a Modern lodge that was based in Halifax and had been warranted in 1789.[189]

Certain Hope Brethren had previously been members of Harmony and it has been theorised by the Yorkshire Masonic historian C. J. Scott that various Bradford Masons under the York Grand Lodge could have gone through a re-making ceremony in the Lodge of Harmony and went on to found Lodge of Hope in Bradford, the location of a gathering of Masons under York in 1713. No evidence has yet come to light of this, but as a theory, it attempts to explain how Lodge of Hope may have come to possess the old York Manuscript Constitution, and how they came to practice the Mark degree. The Brethren of Hope could thus be members of a larger Masonic networking community as a 'Modern' lodge, but with the possession of the old York Manuscript Constitution, they could have the ancient right to practice other degrees.[190]

# THE YORK 'UNION' LODGE NO. 236 AND THE END OF THE YORK GRAND LODGE

William Blanchard became the last surviving member of the York Grand Lodge, and was the custodian of the minutes and documents after its demise. He became the main source of information for Masonic historians in the early nineteenth century, and a number of sources mention him, or a member of his family as supplying documents; local historian G. Benson mentioned that it was a 'Captain Blanchard' who presented the Records of the York Grand Lodge to the York based 'Union' Lodge in 1837,[191] though in the official history of the lodge, William Blanchard himself is cited as presenting many of the records to the Union Lodge in 1817.[192] Blanchard apparently gave the Grand Lodge Board (painted by Thomas Beckwith back in 1778) to a Bro. Turner of the 'Union' Lodge, and Arthur Edward Waite revealed that Blanchard was the source for the mysterious documents seen by Godfrey Higgins and mentioned that Blanchard had given documents and papers to local York historian William Hargrove. Gould in his *History of Freemasonry* also mentions Hargrove seeing the 1780-1792 minute book in the hands of Blanchard in 1819.[193] Whatever the story, like James Miller - the last surviving Mason under the Wigan Grand Lodge over a century later, Blanchard became much sought after for information concerning the York Grand Lodge, as it soon became swathed in Masonic mystery.

In the first minute book of the Manchester based Jerusalem Preceptory, there is an interesting copy letter dated 8 July 1791, which gives an indication of the dire state that the York Grand Lodge was in. The letter from Br. George Kitson of York and addressed to 'Mr. Hassall', concerns the application of warrants for further degrees by the Encampment, and the obvious lack of activity in York:

'...you have so long been disappointed of your warrants. The illness of our G.M. and the absence of our Deputy G. Who has been long in London is the reason of our delay – Bro. Wooley I am told will soon return and as our G.M. is a little better, I hope very soon we shall hold a Chapter and a RE and then the Secy will have orders to prepare and send you the warrants.'

It seems that the lack of communication persisted as on 14 April 1793, five members of the Encampment were nominated to visit 'Mr. Singelair'. This was obviously a reference to Robert Sinclair, and in the July, the expenses of a Brother sent to York were paid, and it seemed that some kind of a discussion took place - either concerning the warrants or to discuss the future of the Encampment in light of the decline of the York Grand Lodge. Either way on 20 May 1795, the Encampment had a new warrant under the Dunkerley Grand Encampment and entered into a new phase in its history.[194]

We can say that the York Grand Lodge, in accordance to the available documentation, continued officially until 1792, but, as we have seen, its last two subordinate lodges lasted slightly longer; the Druidical lodge in Rotherham lasting to around 1795 and the Lodge of Fortitude in Hollinwood, Lancashire, operating perhaps as late as 1802. When

*The York 'Union' Lodge certificate showing the Ouraoboros and the Crypt of the Minster.* (Courtesy of the library, Duncombe Place)

YORK LODGE.
No 236.

In consideration of
the services rendered to
Freemasonry by our

Brother

York                18

and of the high
esteem in which he is held by the Members of the York
Lodge of Ancient, Free and Accepted Masons he was
this day elected an Honorary Member of the York Lodge

W. M.

Dec<sup>r</sup>

Crypt of York Minster

## Friday 18th February 1780.

The Companions of the Honorable Order
of Knights Templars assembled at the
Grand Lodge Room in York pursuant to
Summons.

Present.

⌐□⌐ Francis Smyth — Grand Master
⌐□⌐ Thos. Beckwith. Grand Aid de Camp.
⌐□⌐ John Coupland Deputy Grand Aid de Camp
  ⌐□⌐ John Browne, Scribe
  ⌐□⌐ John Jennings Messenger.
  ⌐□⌐ John Hampston
  ⌐□⌐ John Hassall.

Grand Lodge of Knights Templars was opened and
the Royal Encampment formed and raised And Our
Brother and Companion ⌐□⌐ Francis Smyth
having been duly Elected to and Invested in the High
Duty of Grand Master and Grand Commander of the
of Knights Templars in England was at this Royal
Encampment declared acknowledged and obeyed as
And he nominated for his Officers as follows —

Robert Lakeland, Grand Aid de Camp
Thos. Beckwith, Deputy Grand Aid de Camp
Revd. John Parker, Grand Chaplain
John Jennings, Senior Messenger or Knight of the Watch.
The Junior Messenger to be nominated at a future
                                Encampment.
the Knights unanimously Elected John Browne
to the Office of Scribe.

Brother Francis Clubley having been unanimously approved at a previous Encampment to
be Initiated and made a Knight and Companion
Order of Templars or Knights of the Tabernacle
received Initiated and made a Knight & Companion
accordingly And on Ballott was admitted a Member
to Royal Grand Encampment of all England.

ordered to be

examining the local York based Modern 'Union' Lodge, the influence of the Grand Lodge may have even survived into the early years of the nineteenth century, with some of the surviving York Grand Lodge members, such as Blanchard, the last known Grand Master Edward Wolley, Robert Sinclair and especially the Rev. John Parker, interacting with and visiting the 'Union' Lodge - the 'York' members being well received by a local Modern lodge which had been founded on the principles of union.

According to the history of the York 'Union' Lodge, certain leading members of the York Grand Lodge had subsequently joined the Union Lodge, such as Brother J. Consitt who joined 'after the demise of the York Grand Lodge' and his brother R. Consitt who joined in 1789.[195] However, when the last known Grand Master Edward Wolley visited the York 'Union' Lodge on 27 August 1802, he signed himself as a member of the York Grand Lodge. As we have seen, the Rev. John Parker visited the York 'Union' Lodge a total of 25 times between 1802-1814, and he was regularly referred to in the minutes as the 'Grand Chaplain' to the York Grand Lodge.[196]

Interestingly, with the decline of the York Grand Lodge, the Provincial Grand Lodge of Yorkshire had started to meet regularly once more after December 1803, becoming more pro-active, and in October 1805, the Hon. Lawrence Dundas became Deputy Provincial Grand Master. Dundas had been present at the meeting of the York 'Union' Lodge on 27 August 1802, when Edward Wolley and the Rev. Parker had attended, and Dundas went on to become the first Provincial Grand Master of the newly created Province of the North and East Ridings of Yorkshire, being installed on 14 August 1821.[197]

The large Yorkshire Province had been split in two in 1817, to make it more manageable, a move that in light of the rebellion that was to come in Lancashire, was very wise.

It can be said that the spirit of the York Grand Lodge was still very much alive with the activities of prominent members such as Sinclair, Wolley and the Rev. Parker, who, incidentally, did not join any other lodge. It seemed that the essence of the York Grand Lodge at least, might have indeed continued into the early decades of the nineteenth century, its embers finally dying with the last of its members.

Left: *A page of the minute book showing a Knights Templar meeting.*

Overleaf: *A page from the York Lodge minute book showing the Rev. John Parker and Edward Wolley visiting the lodge in 1802.*

Masters Lodge of Emergency Augt 27 1802

Present Wm Scruton W.M      Thos Edwards
John Seller ... S.W      Benjamin Carr
John Brookbank J.W      Wm Cobb
Edwd Beck Treas:      John Barnard
Wm Gamble Sec, y ...      Wm Steel
Thos Clark .........      Wm Hudson
Geo Whitwell ......      Thos Bradley
Thos Richardson ...      Saml James
Wm Lyth ..........      John Morley
I Weatherill .......      John Bewley
Geo Scruton ......      John Munkman
M Bowman ......      Thos Moor
T Walker ......      Robt Mountain
T Weatherill..      Br Smith
Br Hamilton.

Visitors Edw and Woolley of the Grand Lodge of all England
The Revd John Parker Grand Chaplin to the Grand Lodge of
England

John Watson provincial Grand Secret, y for the County
Din, Peacock of the Appollo Lodge ........
Wr Maxwell of the Rodney Lodge Hull ..........
W Harrison of the Minerva Hull ..........
Br Smith formerly of Hallifax ..........
The Honor Lawerence Dundas ..
Br Price Robinson.

The Minuts of the Last Lodge was redy and Comfirmd
this being don the W Master Rose and Informed the
Bretheren that a Dispenceation from the Provincal
Grand Secret, y had been granted, to Open the Union
Lodge in a Hired Room for that evening in
Inconsequence of Br Seller's House being Engaged
it being the Race Week, the W Master then signifid
that his Room in Blake street was at their service
which was Acceptd, he Then Proposed Sr G Rupel Bart
to be made a Mason 2 by Br Seller 3 by Br Brookbank
in this Lodge the W C M proposed the Hon: & Rev Thomas
Lawerence Dundas as proper person to be made a Mason
in this Lodge 2 by Br Seller and 3 by Br Brookbank
this being a Lose of Emergency, a Ballot was taken for
the Hon, George Henage Lawerence Dundas george Pyson
& the Hon: Revd Thomas Lawerence Dundas and all
Aproved of, the Masters Lodge then Closed and Aprentice
Lodge opened, and they was properly prepaird and
Initiated into the First degree the Charge was given and
the provin, Grand Secrt, y proposed that as Messrs
Dundas was not residents in York they should be Pd,
to the 2 degree or that of Fellow Craft this Motion was
2 by Br Beck and 3 by Br Brookbank the Lodge then Closed

# CONCLUSION

The history of York from the sixteenth century onwards has been intertwined with that of the history of Freemasonry. Indeed, evidence of Freemasonry and Freemasons can be seen throughout York, in the beautiful historical buildings, the artefacts and the manuscripts. There were many taverns and Inns within York that were meeting places for lodges such as the Punch Bowl, which can still be seen, and medieval buildings such as the Merchant Adventurers' Hall which was the scene of Francis Drake's ground-breaking oration in December 1726. From the two historical Masonic Halls situated in York to the many medieval churches associated with local Freemasons, there are many places to visit and to feel the sense of Masonic history in this ancient northern city.

The Minster is indeed the focal point for the medieval stonemasons of York, and is a place that has associations with many Freemasons from the city of York, such as the nineteenth century Minster historian John Browne who was a member of the York 'Union' Lodge and eighteenth century Minster organist John Camidge who was a member of Apollo Lodge. The Minster also reveals windows with Masonic themes, countless stonemasons' marks and has the Crypt, where the York Grand Lodge met; the Crypt becoming a symbol prominently displayed on the Grand Lodge board and on subsequent artwork of the York 'Union' Lodge. Similarly, the nearby Bedern Hall has a recent history with the recently revived York Grand Lodge. There are also the elegant Georgian townhouses of the Bathurst and Fairfax family, the historic printing presses of York, memorials and gravestones and important York landmarks such as Micklegate Bar, all associated with York

Freemasonry and entwined with the social history of the area.

The importance of York Masonry can never be underestimated; as a localised independent Grand Lodge in the eighteenth century, York became the centre of a progressive form of Masonry that spread its influence over the border into Lancashire, an influence that even penetrated London, the practice of five degrees becoming an attractive form of Masonry for Freemasons that wished to freely explore further 'grades'. The use of the 'York' name in regards to Freemasonry during the later eighteenth century seemed to reflect the use of the Edwin legend, with many Antient lodges using the legend. Indeed, a group of 'York' Masons in South Carolina in America wanted to form a Grand Lodge of '*four lodges of ancient York Masons*', three of which held Warrants from the Grand Lodge of Pennsylvania and a lodge that belonged to the '*grand lodge of ancient free masons of England and not to the York Masons*', came together to form the Grand Lodge of South Carolina in 1787.[198]

The 'York' name within Freemasonry still fascinates and has certainly inspired its use in the York Rite, which is a Rite that offers a progressive pathway within Freemasonry for Masons wanting to explore further degrees, such as the Royal Arch, the Mark degree and the Knights Templar degrees, a progression that can be seen in the progressive structure of the York Grand Lodge. The York Rite, which is also popular in Latin American countries such as Mexico and Bolivia, was discussed in detail in *Duncan's Masonic Ritual and Monitor* which was published in the USA in 1866, Duncan stating the purpose of the work being so the Mason could 'progress from grade to grade'.[199] York's famous Freemasons are still celebrated within a social historical context, writers such as Godfrey Higgins, John Browne and Francis Drake, are all still very much respected, their work still being influential in modern times. York deserves its place as a historic centre for Masonry, a centre that still displays its strong Masonic links.

*The Crypt of York Minster was reputedly the meeting place of the York Grand Lodge 'Royal Arch or Templar Encampment on the 27th of May 1778, and was the scene of a reported meeting of the latest revival of the York Grand Lodge, held in June 2008, where the Grand Master received 'The Order of Service to Freemasonry' from the Chancellor of The Grand Loge De France.*
Photo (https://commons.wikimedia.org/wiki/File:The_Crypt,_York_Minster.jpg) by Poliphilo / CC BY (https://creativecommons.org/publicdomain/zero/1.0.0/deed.en)

# NOTES

Notes to **Introduction** (page 7)
1 <http://www.ancientyorklodge.org/> [accessed 29th of April, 2015]
2 <http://www.ancientyork89.org/> [accessed 29th of April, 2015]
3 <http://yorkmexico.org/index.html> [accessed 26th of November, 2014]
4 Information for the Boliviana Rito de York can be found on their website: <http://www.granlogiadebolivia.bo/la-gran-logia-de-bolivia.html> [accessed 26th of June, 2015]

Notes to **York as the Ancient Centre of Northern England** (pages 8-11)
5 Neville Barker Cryer, York Mysteries Revealed, (Hersham: Barker Cryer, 2006), pp.234-5.
6 David Harrison, The York Grand Lodge, (Bury St. Edmunds: Arima Publishing, 2014), pp.15-16.
7 Francis Drake, Eboracum or The History and Antiquities of the City of York, from its Original to the Present Time; together with the History of the Cathedral Church and the Lives of the Archbishops of that See, (London: William Bowyer, 1736), p.241.
8 Ibid, pp.86-7. For a discussion on Drake's portrayal of William the Conqueror as a villain and how York was destroyed and struggled to rebuild its fortunes, see the excellent paper by Rosemary Sweet, 'History and Identity in Eighteenth-Century York: Francis Drake's Eboracum (1736)', in Eighteenth-Century York: Culture, Space and Society, (York: University of York, 2003), pp.14-23, on p.18.
9 See Harrison, York Grand Lodge, pp.45-57.

10 W. J. Hughan. The Old Charges of British Freemasons, (London: Simpkin, Marshall & Co., 1872), pp.5-6.
11 See Godfrey Higgins, Anacalypsis, (Stilwell: Digireads.com Publishing, 2007), pp.767-70. The York MS No. 1 is still in the possession of the York Lodge.
12 Arthur Edward Waite in his Secret Tradition in Freemasonry, (Kessinger, 1997), pp.50-51, stated that Blanchard had given 'all the books and papers' of the York Grand Lodge to William Hargrove, and that Godfrey Higgins from Doncaster, sometime before 1836, went to York and 'applied to the only survivor of the Lodge who shewed me, from the documents which he possessed, that the Druidical Lodge, or Chapter of Royal Arch Masons, or Templar Encampment was held for the last time in the Crypt [of the Cathedral at York] on Sunday, May 27th, 1778.'
13 See Andrew Prescott, 'The Hidden Currents of 1813', The Square, Vol. 40, No. 2, (June 2014), pp.31-2.
14 William Hargrove. History and Description of the Ancient City of York, Vol. I, (York: William Alexander, 1818).
15 R. F. Gould. The History of Freemasonry, Vol.II, (London: Thomas C. Jack, 1883), p.419.

Notes to **An Introduction to the Grand Lodge of all England held at York** (pages 12-15)
16 Part of this piece also appeared in the article by myself in Philalethes: The Journal of Masonic Research & Letters, Vol. 67, No. 1, (Winter, 2014), entitled 'Dr Francis Drake and the Grand Lodge of All England',

pp.6-13.

17 David Harrison. *The Genesis of Freemasonry*, (Hersham: Lewis Masonic, 2009), pp.31-36.

18 Gould. *History of Freemasonry*, pp.407-8. Also see T.B. Whytehead, 'The Relics of the Grand Lodge at York', AQC, Vol.XIII (1900), pp.93-5.

19 Gould. *History of Freemasonry*, pp.407-8, and Whytehead, 'Relics at York', AQC, Vol. XIII, pp.93-5.

20 Gould. *History of Freemasonry*, pp.407-8, and Whytehead, 'Relics at York', AQC, Vol. XIII, pp.93-5.

21 Ibid.

22 Ibid.

23 Anon. *The Antient Constitutions of the Free and Accepted Masons, with a speech deliver'd at the Grand Lodge at York*, (London: B. Creake, 1731), p.20.

24 Neville Barker Cryer. *York Mysteries*, pp.267-8. Barker Cryer certainly supports the view that the Jacobite Rebellion had an effect on the York Grand Lodge, forcing its members to cease their meetings until the political climate had eased somewhat.

25 Anon. *The Antient Constitutions of the Free and Accepted Masons, with a speech deliver'd at the Grand Lodge at York*, (London: B. Creake, 1731), p.20.

26 Thomas Paine. *Origins of Freemasonry*, taken from *The Works of Thomas Paine*, (New York: E. Haskell, 1854), p.217.

27 Gould. *History of Freemasonry*, pp.407-8, and Whytehead, 'Relics at York', AQC, Vol. XIII, pp.93-5.

28 Gould. *History of Freemasonry*, pp.413-5, and Whytehead, 'Relics at York', AQC, Vol. XIII, pp.96-7.

29 Visiting brethren from the Lodge of Fortitude are mentioned in the Minutes of the Lodge of Friendship No. 277, on the 16th of February, 1791 – 23rd of September, 1795, and associated Fortitude brethren are mentioned up until 1811. Masonic Hall, Rochdale. Not listed.

30 G. Benson. *John Browne 1793-1877, Artist and the Historian of York Minster*. (York: Yorkshire Philosophical Society, 1918), p.5.

31 The York Grand Lodge Minute Books dating from March 17, 1712 and ending August 23, 1792 are in the possession of the York 'Union' Lodge. There are no Minutes however from 1734-1761.

32 Wood. *York Lodge No. 236*, p.20.

33 Gould. *History of Freemasonry*, pp.419-21. Also, see Waite, New Encyclopaedia of Freemasonry, Vol.II, p.482. Gould stated that the 1780-92 volume of Minutes from the York Grand Lodge was missing at the time of his writing. As stated above, these Minutes can currently be found at Freemasons Hall, York.

Notes to **The Mysteries of Micklegate** (pages 16-19)

34 Neville Barker Cryer. *York Mysteries*, p.306.

35 Fitzroy Maclean. *Bonnie Prince Charlie*, (Edinburgh: Canongate, 1989), pp.117-131.

36 See Maclean, *Bonnie Prince Charlie*, pp.246-259.

37 See P.M. Dunn, 'Dr John Burton (1710-1771) of York and his obstetric treatise', *in Arch Dis Child Fetal Neonatal*, 84, (2001), F74-f76, which presents a fine critique of Burton's essay on Midwifery.

Notes to **Taverns, Inns, Coffee Houses and Booksellers associated with York Freemasonry** (pages 20-24)

38 Gould, *History of Freemasonry*, Vol.II, pp.413-5, and Whytehead, 'Relics at York', AQC, Vol.XIII, pp.96-7.

39 See Barker Cryer, *York Mysteries Revealed*, p.327, taken from the York Grand Lodge minute book 1761-1774, the proposed letter to the Grand Lodge of London written in December 1767 by the Grand Secretary D. Lambert, Duncombe Place, York.

40 See Tate Wilkinson, *Memoirs of His own Life*, (York: Wilson, Spence and Mawman, 1790).

41 See <http://www.british-history.ac.uk/vch/yorks/city-of-york/pp537-541#h3-0003> [accessed 20 April 2015]

42  Blanchard published a sermon by the Grand Chaplain of York: John Parker, Vicar of St. Helen's York, *A sermon, preached in the parish-church of Rotherham, before the Most Worshipful Grand Master of the most ancient Grand Lodge of all England ... and the newly constituted Rotherham Druidical Lodge of Free and Accepted Masons, December 22, 1778*, (York: W. Blanchard and Co., 1779).

43  See Joseph Smith, *A Descriptive Catalogue of Friends' Books, or Books written by the Members of the Society of Friends, commonly called Quakers*, (London: Joseph Smith, 1867), p.464.

44  A concise history of the *York Chronicle* is given in *Hargrove, History and Description of the Ancient City of York*, p.261. Arthur Edward Waite in his Secret Tradition in Freemasonry, p.51, stated that Blanchard had given 'all the books and papers' of the York Grand Lodge to William Hargrove.

45  Hargrove. *History and Description of the Ancient City of York*, p.261.

46  Charles Henry Timperley. *A Dictionary of Printers and Printing*, (London: Johnson, 1839), p.945.

47  'Newspapers', A History of the County of York: the City of York (1961), pp.537-541. URL: <http://www.british-history.ac.uk/report.aspx?compid=36391> [accessed: 19 May 2012]

48  See Bernadette Bensaude-Vincent and Isabelle Stengers, *A History of Chemistry*, (Cambridge MA: Harvard University Press, 1997), pp.59-60. See also Harrison, *Genesis of Freemasonry*, pp.127-8.

49  See Harrison. *York Grand Lodge*, p.52.

50  Barker Cryer. *York Mysteries*, p.253.

51  See <http://goodhumour.laurencesternetrust.org.uk/history/members-of-the-club/> [accessed 22nd of August, 2013]. Two recently discovered minute books belonging to the Good Humour Club; a minute book dating from 1743, the other dating from 1781, led to research conducted by Hugh Murray for the Laurence Sterne Trust in 2013, and a subsequent exhibition regarding the history

of the club was held at Shandy Hall during the summer of that year.

52  See Harrison. *Genesis of Freemasonry*, p.140 and p.173.

53  Barker Cryer. *York Mysteries*, p.254.

54  Ibid. p.256.

55  Ibid., pp.253-4.

56  Ibid., p.254.

**Notes to The Merchant Adventures' Hall, the Guildhall and the Merchant Taylors Hall** (pages 25-26)

57  G.Y. Johnson, *The Merchant Adventurers' Hall and its Connection with Freemasonry*, (A paper read before the Leeds Masters' Association, 22nd June, 1935), pp.1-3.

58  Anon., *The Antient Constitutions of the Free and Accepted Masons, with a speech deliver'd at the Grand Lodge at York*, (London: B. Creake, 1731), pp.19-20.

59  Knoop, Jones and Hamer, *Early Masonic Pamphlets*, (1945), p.196.

60  Shawn Eyer, 'Drake's Oraton of 1726' in *Philalethes: The Journal of Masonic Research & Letters*, Vol. 67, No. 1, (Winter, 2014), p.14.

61  Anon., *The Antient Constitutions of the Free and Accepted Masons, with a speech deliver'd at the Grand Lodge at York*, (London: B. Creake, 1731), p.21-22.

62  Johnson, *The Merchant Adventurers' Hall and its Connection with Freemasonry*, p.4.

63  Ibid., pp.3-24.

64  See <http://www.merchant-taylors-york.org/> [accessed 7th of July, 2015]

65  See David Harrison. *The Genesis of Freemasonry*, (Hersham: Lewis Masonic, 2009), pp.56-7, where I put forward that the medieval Mystery Plays, which revealed moralistic themes from the Bible stories, may have been an influence on Masonic ritual.

66  See <http://www.yorkmysteryplays.co.uk/> [accessed 7th of July, 215]

67   N.B. Cryer. *Masonic Halls of England: The North*, (Shepperton: Lewis Masonic, 1989), pp.129-135.

68   Ibid.

69   Ibid.

70   The Beckwith Manuscripts, Ref: MS60-79, Yorkshire Archaeological Society.

71   See G.Y. Johnson. *The Subordinate Lodges Constituted by the York Grand Lodge*, (Margate: W. J. Parrett, 1942), p.44.

72   Ibid.

73   Ibid, p.45.

74   Ibid., p.74.

75   York MS No. 1, Duncombe Place, York.

76   Barker Cryer. *York Mysteries Revealed*, pp.156-7.

77   Ibid, p.vii.

78   The version of the 'Old Charges' written by Edward Sankey are preserved in the British Museum, the document being known as the Sloane MS No. 3848, see Hughan, *The Old Charges of British Freemasons*, p.8.

79   For a further description of the York MS No. 1 see Hughan, *The Old Charges of British Freemasons*, pp.5-6. Hughan mentions that the document was presented to the York Grand Lodge by Drake in 1736, but Barker Cryer mentioned that the date was 1732; see Barker Cryer, *York Mysteries*, p.156. However, William Hargrove in his *History and Description of the Ancient City of York* gives the date as 1738, which is discussed in H. Poole and F.R. Worts, *"Yorkshire" Old Charges of Masons*, (York: Ben Johnson & Co. Ltd, 1935), p.110, where Poole and Worts suggest it could be 1736 or 1738. When York Lodge archivist David Taylor and I examined the written text on the reverse of one of the four sheets of parchment that comprise the MS No. 1, the ink was faded somewhat, but we both agreed that the last digit looked like a six. If this is correct then the manuscript was given to the Grand Lodge as late as 1736, and was thus still very much in operation at that time.

80   Hughan. *Old Charges of British Freemasons*, p.6. Hughan mentions that the grandfather of Dr Francis Drake wrote a Diary of the Siege.

81   See Barker Cryer. *York Mysteries Revealed*, p.189. For a comprehensive list of the Sheriffs and Lord Mayors of York see Hargrove, *History and Description of the Ancient City of York*, Vol. I, p.327.

82   York MS No. 4, Duncombe Place, York. For a description of the York MS No. 4 see also Hughan, *Old Charges of British Freemasons*, pp.15-16.

83   Ibid. For the Tees Valley associations of the six men named in the York MS No. 4, see Barker Cryer, *York Mysteries*, p.191.

84   York MS No. 4.

85   Hughan, *Old Charges of British Freemasons*, pp.15-16.

86   Ibid., p.16.

87   Anon., *Jachin and Boaz, a New Edition*, (London: W. Nicoll, 1785), p.9. Also see David Harrison, *A Quick Guide to Freemasonry*, (Hersham: Lewis Masonic, 2013), p.15.

88   Anon., Memoir of the Lady Freemason, (Cork: John Day, 1995), p.12.

89   York MS No. 7, displaying minutes of lodge meetings dating from the 19th of March, 1712 until the 4th of May, 1730, Duncombe Place, York. For a transcription of these minutes see Gould, *History of Freemasonry*, Vol.II, pp.271-4 and pp.401-4.

90   Ibid. A St. John's Lodge meeting is also referred to on the 24th of June, 1729, the festival of John the Baptist.

91   Ibid.

92   See the website of the York Lodge <http://www.yorklodge236.org.uk/page8.html> [accessed 7th of July, 2015]

93   See Lane's Masonic Records online: <http://www.hrionline.ac.uk/lane/record.php?ID=10646> [accessed 21st of March, 2015]

94   See <http://www.britishlistedbuildings.co.uk/en-463012-castlegate-house-and-attached-railings-> [accessed 21st of March, 2015]

95   See <http://www.alcuinlodge.org.uk/> [accessed 21st of March, 2015]

96   See <http://www.agricolalodge1991.org.
     uk/> [accessed 21st of March, 2015]


Notes to **Civic buildings associated with York**
(pages 34-38)

97   See Harrison, *York Grand Lodge*, p.27.

98   Ralph Harrington, 'The Plasterwork of
     the Great Staircase at Fairfax House, York:
     towards an iconographical and historical
     analysis', (2012), [Online] Available from:
     <http://www.academia.edu/3149237/
     The_plasterwork_of_the_Great_Staircase_
     at_Fairfax_House_York_towards_an_
     iconographical_and_historical_analysis_
     part_1_text_> [accessed 27th of July, 2015]

99   For a critical appraisal of Carr's designs see
     Albert E. Richardson, *Monumental Classic
     Architecture in Greta Britain and Ireland*,
     (New York: Dover Publications Inc., 2001),
     p.xvii.

100  For the lodge at the Cock and Bottle,
     London, see John Lane's Masonic Records
     of England and Wales 1717-1894 online:
     <http://www.freemasonry.dept.shef.ac.uk/
     lane/> [accessed 17th of July, 2007] and John
     Pine, *A List of Regular Lodges according to
     their Seniority & Constitution*. Printed for
     & Sold by I. Pine, Engraver, (London: Little
     Brittain end in Aldergate Street, 1735).

101  See Pamela Denman Kingsbury, 'Boyle,
     Richard, third earl of Burlington and
     fourth earl of Cork (1694-1753)', Oxford
     Dictionary of National Biography, Oxford
     University Press, 2004; online edition, Jan
     2008 <http://www.oxforddnb.com/view/
     article/3136> [accessed 19th of June, 2014]

102  For more information on the possible
     Masonic influences on Chiswick House see
     Ricky Pound, 'Chiswick House - a Masonic
     Temple?', in Gillian Clegg (eds.), *Brentford
     & Chiswick Local History Journal*, Number
     16, 2007, pp.4-7.

103  Harrison, *Genesis of Freemasonry*, pp.86-
     108.

104  Barker Cryer, *York Mysteries*, p.288.

105  See Sybil Rosenfeld, *Strolling Players
     and Drama in the Provinces 1660-1765*,
     (Cambridge: Cambridge University Press,

1939), pp.156-158.

106  Extracts from Frodsham's 'charge' can
     be seen in Barker Cryer, *York Mysteries*,
     pp.307-9. Taken from the *Newcastle Free-
     masons Companion of 1777*.

107  For Thomas Dundas see *Annual Report of
     the Council of the Yorkshire Philosophical
     Society*, (Thomas Wilson & Sons, 1832),
     p.39.

108  *Annual Report of the Council of the
     Yorkshire Philosophical Society for 1825*,
     (York: W. Alexander & Son, 1826), p.36 &
     p.37.

109  *Annual Report of the Council of the
     Yorkshire Philosophical Society for 1830*,
     (York: W. Alexander & Son, 1830), pp.44-
     48.

110  See Harrison, *Transformation of
     Freemasonry*, pp.84-96.

111  See Richard Carlile, *Manual of
     Freemasonry*, (Croydon: New Temple
     Press, 1912), and Thomas Paine, *Origins
     of Freemasonry*, in *The Works of Thomas
     Paine*, (New York: E. Haskell, 1854).


Notes to **The Minster and other Churches
in and around York associated with
Freemasons** (pages 39-46)

112  Minute Books of the York 'Union' Lodge
     No. 236, number 10 and 11. See also Barker
     Cryer, *York Mysteries*, p.351-2.

113  Minutes of the Union Lodge, York, No. 236,
     Book 10, January 1796-December 1808,
     10th of March, 1802. Duncombe Place,
     York.

114  Ibid, 1st of June, 1802. The entry refers to a
     '*Br. Sinclair*' honouring the lodge with his
     company, but it seems obvious that this is
     Robert Sinclair who is being referred to,
     and Masonic historian and Librarian of the
     York 'Union' Lodge G.Y. Johnson indicated
     this confidently in his transcription of the
     minutes. There was also a '*Bro. Sinclair*'
     who visited the Lennox Lodge No. 123,
     in Richmond, in July, 1812. Barker Cryer
     states that Sinclair visited the York 'Union'
     Lodge twice in 1802; see Barker Cryer, *York
     Mysteries*, p.351.

115 Minutes of the Union Lodge, York, No. 236, Book 10, January 1796-December 1808, 27th of August, 1802. Duncombe Place, York.

116 Wood, *York Lodge*, p.18. The death of the Rev. Parker is reported in the *York Courant* on Monday, the 19th of June, 1815, and his burial on Monday, the 25th of June, 1815.

117 Barker Cryer, *York Mysteries*, pp.434-5.

118 John Marsden, *The Illustrated Bede*, (London: Macmillan, 1989), p.16.

119 Taken from J. Raine, (ed.), Fabric Rolls of York Minster (1360-1639, with an Appendix, 1165-1704), Surtees Society, Vol. 35, (London: Mitchell and Son, 1859), pp.171-2. See also Barker Cryer, *York Mysteries*, p.82. Barker Cryer comments on the masons' lodge at York Minster and how it was used, presenting a brief translation of the Latin from the Rolls.

120 Raine, p.171 and p.181.

121 Ibid., p.17. See also Barker Cryer, *York Mysteries*, pp.82-3 and pp.125-6. See also D. Knoop and G.P. Jones, *Genesis of Freemasonry*, (Manchester: Manchester University Press, 1947), p.37. Knoop and Jones also discuss the lodge at York Minster based on Raine's work on the Fabric Rolls.

122 Raine, p.17. Barker Cryer in his *York Mysteries*, incorrectly puts this year as 1399.

123 Ibid., p.50.

124 For a list of Sheriff's and Lord Mayors of York see Hargrove, *History and Description of the Ancient City of York*, Vol. I, p.319-20. See also Raine, pp.91-2 and p.97. He is described as 'magistri Drawswerd'.

125 W.H. Rylands, 'Freemasonry in Lancashire & Cheshire in the 17th Century', LCHS, (1898), pp.131-202, on p.135-6.

126 Neville Barker Cryer, 'The Grand Lodge of All England at York and its Practices', see <http://www.lodgehope337.org.uk/lectures/cryer%20S02.PDF> [accessed 21st of July, 2009]

127 Barker Cryer, York Mysteries, pp.163-4 and pp.179-180. Barker Cryer refers to a relatively small list of seven men listed as either '*freemaysons*' or '*masons*', compiled by G.Y. Johnson that became freemen of York between 1619-1691. Barker Cryer suggested that by 1700, the non-operatives had used the new name of 'freemayson' while the operatives had reverted to being called 'mason'.

128 Wood, *York Lodge*, p.118 & p.125.

129 George Benson, *John Browne 1793-1877 Artist and Historian of York Minster*, (York: York Philosophical Society, 1918), pp.4-6.

130 Ibid., p.3.

131 Ibid., p.7.

132 Ibid., p.9.

133 David Griffiths, *The Camidges of York: Five Generations of a Musical Family*, (York: Borthwick Papers, 2010), pp.9-10.

134 The records of Bedern Hall, York, reveal that a meeting did take place on this date, organised by the Grand Secretary Peter J. Clatworthy. The existing manager of the Hall still remembers the meeting as a dinner event with attendees from all over the country.

135 See Trevor W. McKeown, 'An historical outline of freemasons online', Grand Lodge of British Columbia and Yukon, (2008), p.31. McKeown certainly notes the coincidence with the founding of the independent Regular Grand Lodge of England in January 2005 and the founding of the Grand Lodge of All England later that year. Indeed, correspondence between myself and Rui Gabirro, who was a leading member of the Regular Grand Lodge of England, confirmed that the Masons behind the formation of the Grand Lodge of All England had been involved with Masons from the Regular Grand Lodge of England, which also incidentally, uses the Edwin legend on its website.

136 See <http://freemasonsfordummies.blogspot.co.uk/2007/11/another-lodge-appears.html> [accessed 4th of April, 2014]. The website is managed by Christopher Hodapp, the US based author of Freemasons for Dummies.

137 The Grand Loge De France is not recognised by the UGLE, but they do have a lodge which meets in London called The White Swan Lodge No. 1348: <http://

www.thewhiteswan.org/> [accessed 12th of March, 2014]. The Grand Loge De France and the 'revived' Grand Lodge of All England had exchanged Treaties of Amity the previous year.

138 Correspondence between the author and the Grand Master John Gordon Graves, dated the 29th of March, 2014.

139 The Brethren of the 'revived' York Grand Lodge mentioned online were Grand Master John Gordon Graves; Grand Secretary Peter J. Clatworthy; Grand Chancellor Richard Martin Young and the first WM of the St John's Lodge in Dayton, Ohio, Daniel Scherr. There have been many independent Grand Lodges in the US that are not recognised by the regular Masonic bodies, and the 'revived' York Grand Lodge seems to have approached Freemasons for possible recruitment from this independent Masonic community; indeed, Scherr had previously been a member of two of these Grand Lodges in the US, and from correspondence between myself and Jeff Peace, an ex-Freemason from Georgia who was once linked to the independent Halcyon Lodge in Ohio, he recalled being approached by the 'revived' York Grand Lodge with an offer to join, but turned it down.

140 See MQ, Issue 17, April 2006, UGLE Publications. <http://www.mqmagazine. co.uk/issue-17/p-05.php> [accessed 12th of March, 2014]. Only two members are referred to as being involved.

141 See <http://www.bedernhall.co.uk/> [accessed 5th of March, 2015]

Notes to **Wider considerations: country estates and halls associated with York Freemasons** (pages 47-48)

142 <http://www. barwickinelmethistoricalsociety.com/7428. html> [accessed 28th of January, 2013]

143 See <www.parlington.co.uk> [accessed 4th of April, 2015] The website is dedicated to preserving the memory of Palington Hall and the Gascoigne family.

144 John Burke, *A Genealogical and Heraldic History of the Commoners of Great Britain and Ireland*, Vol. I, (London: Henry Colburn, 1834), pp.611-613.

145 Ibid.

146 G.E. Cokayne; with Vicary Gibbs, H.A. Doubleday, Geoffrey H. White, Duncan Warrand and Lord Howard de Walden, (ed.), *The Complete Peerage of England, Scotland, Ireland, Great Britain and the United Kingdom, Extant, Extinct or Dormant*, new ed., 13 volumes in 14 (1910-1959; reprint in 6 volumes, Gloucester: Alan Sutton Publishing, 2000), volume II, p.178. See also <http://www.thepeerage. com/e290.htm> [accessed 21st of June, 2012]

147 L.G. Pine, *The New Extinct Peerage 1884-1971: Containing Extinct, Abeyant, Dormant and Suspended Peerages With Genealogies and Arms* (London: Heraldry Today, 1972), pp.231-232. See also <http:// thepeerage.com/p24141.htm#i2414086> [accessed 21st of June, 2012] and <http:// www.historyofparliamentonline.org/ volume/1690-1715/member/robinson-sir-william-1655-1736> [accessed 21st of June, 2012]

Notes to **Lodges under York and other old Torkshire lodges of interest** (pages 49-57)

148 Anon., York Working Masonic Ritual Compiled from Manuscript Records in the Possession of the York Lodge No. 236, (York: Ben Johnson & Co. Ltd, 1936).

149 Anon., *A Ritual of Craft Masonry 'Humber Use'*, (Hull: Privately Printed, 1988).

150 See <http://www.humber57.org.uk/> [accessed 26th of June, 2015]

151 T.W. Hanson, *The Lodge of Probity No.61, 1738-1938*, (Halifax: The Lodge of Probity, 1938), pp.49-50.

152 See Herbert Crossley, *The History of the Lodge of Probity No. 61*, (Hull: M.C. Peck & Son, 1888).

153 Gould, *History of Freemasonry*, Vol.II, pp.413-5, and Whytehead, 'Relics at York', AQC, Vol.XIII, pp.96-7.

154 See the MS. Roll of the List of the Members names of that Revived the Antient Grand Lodge of All England in 1761and of all who has been made Masons therein since. Duncombe Place, York.

155 York Grand Lodge minute book 1761-1774, 28th of September, 1767. Duncombe Place, York.

156 Ibid., 27th of December, 1770. Also see Barker Cryer, *York Mysteries*, pp.329-331.

157 Extracts from a Minute Book of the Lodge at Scarborough, which mentions six meetings in 1762 and one meeting in 1768, taken from a foolscap sheet held at Duncombe Place, York. Also see Barker Cryer, *York Mysteries*, pp.357-360.

158 York Grand Lodge minute book 1761-1774, 31st of July, 1769. Duncombe Place, York. Also see Barker Cryer, *York Mysteries*, p.328.

159 Barker Cryer, *York Mysteries*, pp.361-2.

160 Lane's Masonic Records <http://freemasonry.dept.shef.ac.uk/lane/> [accessed 9th of June, 2012]

161 Armstrong, *History of Freemasonry in Cheshire*, p.309.

162 Barker Cryer, *York Mysteries*, pp.362-3.

163 Armstrong, *History of Freemasonry in Cheshire*, p.309.

164 John Parker, Vicar of St. Helen's York, *A sermon, preached in the parish-church of Rotherham, before the Most Worshipful Grand Master of the most ancient Grand Lodge of all England ... and the newly constituted Rotherham Druidical Lodge of Free and Accepted Masons, December 22, 1778*, (York: W. Blanchard and Co., 1779).

165 Hassall's letter to the York Grand Lodge is held at Duncombe Place, listed as MS No. 83. The letter is transcribed in Harrison, *York Grand Lodge*, p.123.

166 Beckwith's letter to the York Grand Lodge is held at Duncombe Place, listed as MS No. 67. The letter is transcribed in Harrison, *York Grand Lodge*, p.125-7.

167 Johnson, Subordinate Lodges, p.50.

168 The antagonism between the two Grand Lodges had reached a new height at this time, as seen in the letter from Beckwith to the York Grand Lodge.

169 The minute book of the North Nottinghamshire Lodge No. 587, which also includes in the latter half of the same book the minutes of the Phoenix Lodge, is kept at Duncombe Place, York. The North Nottinghamshire Lodge has minutes dating from the 30th of April, 1792 – 3rd of February, 1808, the remaining Brethren then forming the Phoenix Lodge at Rotherham which has minutes dating from the 22nd July, 1808 – 30th of August 1819. According to John Lane's Masonic Records, the North Nottinghamshire Lodge was discontinued c.1803, and the Rotherham based Phoenix Lodge No.533 was consecrated in 1808, being finally erased in 1838.

170 The minute book of the North Nottinghamshire Lodge No. 587, 22nd June, 1792, p.15. Duncombe Place. Not listed.

171 Ibid., 10th of July, 1795, p.70.

172 Ibid., pp.70-1.

173 Ibid. The four Druidical Brethren mentioned in the list are James Wilkinson - WM, Matthew Dixon, Joseph Flint - Treasurer, and Joseph Medlam. The Rev. Broadbent had off course also joined North Nottinghamshire a number of years before.

174 Ibid., the Inventory being made in July, 1808. For a transcribed version of the Inventory see Johnson, *Subordinate Lodges*, p.74-5. Johnson puts forward that as the Inventory contains so many items; the additional list consisted of the furniture 'taken over from the Druidical Lodge'.

175 See Arthur Edward Waite, *Secret Tradition in Freemasonry*, (Kessinger, 1997), p.50-51. See also Barker Cryer, *York Mysteries*, p.380.

176 Barker Cryer, *York Mysteries*, pp.426-9.

177 Ibid.

178 Ibid., p.461-462. Richard Garland was however still in contact with certain Brethren as he attended a Provincial meeting at the Merchant Adventurers' Hall in York on the 26th of August, 1789, which included a number of Brethren from Apollo as Principal Officers.

179 Ibid., pp.460-465.

180 Ibid., p.463.

181 Correspondence between the Lodge of Probity and the York 'Union' Lodge mentioned in the Minutes of the Union Lodge, York, No. 236, Book 10, 5th of September, 1803. Duncombe Place, York.

182 There are no minute books for the Apollo Lodge after 1788, though there is evidence they continued to meet; Apollo member and ex-'Yorkite' Thomas Thackray became Deputy Provincial Grand Master after Garland, and Thackray seemed to hold the Office until his death in 1793, and John Watson - initiated into Apollo in 1783, served as Provincial Grand Treasurer, then as *Provincial Grand Secretary*, appearing as a frequent visitor to the York 'Union' Lodge (though never becoming a member) until his death in 1815. An example of Watson listed as 'Provincial Grand Secretary' while visiting York 'Union', along with another visitor from Apollo, can be seen in the Minutes of the Union Lodge, York, No. 236, Book 10, 27th of August, 1802. Duncombe Place, York. The Apollo Lodge's number on the Grand Lodge roll was changed a number of times; its original number was No. 450, becoming No. 357 in 1780, and No. 358 in 1781. In 1792 it became No. 290, and after the union of 1813, it was given No. 368.

183 See the letter by Beckwith, MS No. 67. Duncombe Place, York.

184 Paul Kleber Monod, *Solomon's Secret Arts: The Occult in the Age of Enlightenment*, (Yale: Yale University Press, 2013), p.259. See also George S. Draffen, 'Some Further Notes on the Rite of Seven Degrees in London', AQC, Vol 68, (1955), pp.94-110. For discussion on possible evolution of the 'Rite', see John Hamill & R.A. Gilbert, *World Freemasonry: An Illustrated History*, (London: The Aquarian Press, 1991), pp.58-73.

185 See Barker Cryer, *York Mysteries*, p.374.

186 Hughan, *Old Charges of British Freemasons*, p.12. Also see <http://www.rgle.org.uk/The%20old%20charges%20of%20British%20Freemasons%201872.pdf> [accessed 30th of May, 2012]

187 See Waite, *Secret Tradition in Freemasonry*, pp.46-7. See also <http://www.markmastermasonscornwall.org.uk/history-of-mark-master-masons> [accessed 30th of May, 2012]

188 See Bernard H. Springett, The Mark Degree, (London: A. Lewis, 1968), pp.15-17. Springett comments in the history section of the book that early Mark Masonry was worked in Yorkshire, and presents evidence that it was also practiced in the Marquis of Granby Lodge No. 124 in Durham, in 1773. Springett also theorises that the Mark degree may have been taken to the south of England by Thomas Dunkerley.

189 For information on the Lodge of Harmony in Halifax, which still meets today in Huddersfield, see Hanson, *Lodge of Probity*, pp.124-125.

190 C.J. Scott, 'The Tradition of The Old York T. I. Lodge of Mark Master Masons: An enquiry into early Freemasonry at Bradford and neighborhood 1713-1873'. A paper given before the Old York T.I. Lodge at Bradford on November 28th, 1911. Scott was the Chaplain to the Old York T.I. Lodge. <http://www.bradford.ac.uk/webofhiram/?section=york_rite&page=tradoldyork.html> [accessed 30th of October, 2013]

Notes to **The York 'Union' Lodge No 236 and the end of the York Grand Lodge** (pages 58-62)

191 G. Benson, *John Browne 1793-1877, Artist and the Historian of York Minster*. (York: Yorkshire Philosophical Society, 1918), p.5.

192 Wood, *York Lodge*, p.33.

193 Gould, *History of Freemasonry*, Vol.II, p.419.

194 Shepherd & Lane, *Jerusalem Preceptory No. 5*, pp.26-7.

195 Wood, *York Lodge*, p.31 and p.122.

196  Minute Books of the York 'Union' Lodge No. 236, number 10 and 11. See also Barker Cryer, *York Mysteries*, p.351-2.

197  Albert Morton, Lennox Lodge No.123, (Richmond: 1947), pp.15-21. The Hon. Lawrence Dundas (became a joining member of the York 'Union' Lodge in September 1802 and a subscribing member of the Lennox Lodge (based in Richmond, Yorkshire) in December 1830. The Dundas family became embedded with nineteenth and Twentieth century English Freemasonry; the Hon. Thomas Dundas (afterwards the 2nd Earl of Zetland) becoming Provincial Grand Master of the North and East Ridings of Yorkshire in 1834, and serving as Grand Master from 1844-1870.

198  See Harrison, *York Grand Lodge*, p.106.

199  Malcolm C. Duncan, *Duncan's Masonic Ritual and Monitor*, (Forgotten Books: 2008), p.1.

# YORK LODGE, No. 236.

CRYPT OF YORK MINSTER.
Where the Freemasons anciently held their Assemblies

# BIBLIOGRAPHY

**Published Primary Source Material**

Anderson, James, *The Constitutions of The Free-Masons*, (London: Senex, 1723).

Anderson, James, *The New Book of Constitutions of the Antient and Honourable Fraternity of Free and Accepted Masons*, (London: Ward and Chandler, 1738).

Anderson, James, *The Constitutions of the Antient and Honourable Fraternity of Free and Accepted Masons*, Revised by John Entick MA, (London: J. Scott, 1756).

Anderson, James, *Constitutions of the Antient and Honourable Fraternity of Free and Accepted Masons*, (London: G. Kearsly, 1769).

Anon., *The Antient Constitutions of the Free and Accepted Masons, with a speech deliver'd at the Grand Lodge at York*, (London: B. Creake, 1731).

Anon., *Three Distinct Knocks*, (London, 1760).

Anon., *Jachin and Boaz; or an Authentic Key To the Door of Free-Masonry, Both Antient and Modern*, (London: W. Nicoll, St. Paul's Church-Yard, 1763).

*Annual Report of the Council of the Yorkshire Philosophical Society for 1825*, (York: W. Alexander & Son, 1826).

*Annual Report of the Council of the Yorkshire Philosophical Society for 1830*, (York: W. Alexander & Son, 1830).

*Annual Report of the Council of the Yorkshire Philosophical Society*, (Thomas Wilson & Sons, 1832).

Carlile, Richard, *Manual of Freemasonry*, (Croydon: New Temple Press, 1912).

Dermott, Laurence, *Ahiman Rezon*, (London, 1756).

Dermott, Laurence, *Ahiman Rezon, or a help to all that are, or would be Free and Accepted Masons*, Second Edition, (London: Sold by Br. Robert Black, 1764).

Dermott, Laurence, *Ahiman Rezon or a Help to all that are, or would be Free and Accepted Masons (with many additions)*, Third Edition, (London: Printed for James Jones, 1778).

Drake, Francis, *Eboracum or The History and Antiquities of the City of York, from its Original to the Present Time; together with the History of the Cathedral Church and the Lives of the Archbishops of that See*, (London: William Bowyer, 1736).

Drake, Francis, *Eboracum*, (York: Wilson and Spence, 1788).

Duncan, Malcolm C., *Duncan's Masonic Ritual and Monitor*, (Forgotten Books: 2008).

Hargrove, William, History and Description of the Ancient City of York: comprising all the most interesting information already published in Drake's Eboracum, (York: William Alexander, 1818).

Higgins, Godfrey, *Anacalypsis*, (Stilwell: Digireads.com Publishing, 2007).

Paine, Thomas, *The Works of Thomas Paine*, (New York: E. Haskell, 1854).

Parker, John, *Vicar of St. Helen's York, A sermon, preached in the parish-church of Rotherham, before the Most Worshipful Grand Master of the most ancient Grand Lodge of all England ... and the newly constituted Rotherham*

*Druidical Lodge of Free and Accepted Masons, December 22, 1778*, (York: W. Blanchard and Co., 1779).

Preston, William, *Illustrations of Masonry*, (London: Whittaker, Treacher & Co., 1829).

Ramsden Riley, J., *The Yorkshire Lodges: A Century of Yorkshire Freemasonry*, (Leeds: Thomas C. Jack, 1885).

Smith, Joseph, *A Descriptive Catalogue of Friends' Books, or Books written by the Members of the Society of Friends, commonly called Quakers*, (London: Joseph Smith, 1867).

Sterne, Laurence, *The Life and Opinions of Tristram Shandy, Gentleman*, (London: R. & J. Dodsley, 1760).

Timperley, Charles Henry, *A Dictionary of Printers and Printing*, (London: Johnson, 1839).

Webb, Thomas Smith, *Webb's Freemason's Monitor*, (Cincinnati: C. Moore, 1865).

Wilkinson, Tate, *Memoirs of His own Life*, (York: Wilson, Spence and Mawman, 1790).

Wilkinson, Tate, *The Wandering Patentee, Or A History of the Yorkshire Theatres From 1770 to the Present Time*, (York: Wilson, Spence and Mawman, 1795).

*The theatrical inquisitor, or, Monthly mirror*, Volume 12, (London: C. Chapple, 1818).

Burials for St. Mary's Church, Oldham, Jonathan Raynor, 14th of April, 1811, Source Film No. 1656225, Ref No. 6.

**Lodge Histories**

Brown, J., *Masonry in Wigan being a brief history of the Lodge of Antiquity No. 178, Wigan, originally No. 235*, (Wigan: R. Platt, Standishgate and Millgate, 1882).

Crossley, Herbert, *The History of the Lodge of Probity No. 61*, (Hull: M.C. Peck & Son, 1888).

Morton, Albert, *A Brief History of Freemasonry in Richmond, Yorkshire, Compiled from the records of the Lennox Lodge, No. 123, and other sources*, (Richmond: Thomas Spencer, 1911).

Morton, Albert, *Lennox Lodge, No. 123*, (Richmond: 1947).

F. C. Shepherd & M. P. Lane, *Jerusalem Preceptory No. 5. Bi-Centenary History 1786-1986*, (Manchester: Published privately by the Preceptory, 1986).

Wood, Robert Leslie, *York Lodge No. 236, formerly The Union Lodge, the be-centennial history 1777-1977*, (York: Published privately by the lodge, 1977).

**Secondary Sources**

Armstrong, John, *History of Freemasonry in Cheshire*, (London: Kenning, 1901).

Ayres, Philip J., *Classical Culture and the Idea of Rome in Eighteenth-Century England*, (Cambridge: Cambridge University Press, 1997).

Barker Cryer, Neville, *Masonic Halls of England: The North*, (Shepperton: Lewis Masonic, 1989).

Barker Cryer, Neville, *York Mysteries Revealed*, (Hersham: Barker Cryer, 2006).

Benson, G., *John Browne 1793-1877, Artist and the Historian of York Minster*, (York: Yorkshire Philosophical Society, 1918).

Gould, Robert Freke, *History of Freemasonry, Vol. I-III*, (London: Thomas C. Jack, 1883).

Gould, Robert Freke, *The Concise History of Freemasonry*, (New York: Dover Publications, 2007).

Griffiths, David, The Camidges of York: Five Generations of a Musical Family, (York: Borthwick Papers, 2010).

Hamill, John, & Gilbert, R.A., *World Freemasonry: An Illustrated History*, (London: The Aquarian Press, 1991).